PEARSON

REALITY CENTRAL

Real World Writing Journal

PEARSON

Upper Saddle River, New Jersey • Boston, Massachusetts
Chandler, Arizona • Glenview, Illinois • Shoreview, Minnesota

13-digit ISBN: 978-0-13-367512-2

10-digit ISBN: 0-13-367512-2

15   V011   17 16 15

TABLE OF CONTENTS

ABOUT YOUR BOOK

The What and Why of This Book

This book is designed to help you develop strategies you can use while learning about writing, grammar, usage, and vocabulary. While you write and work with vocabulary, you will return to the articles in your Student Anthology. You will think more deeply about the Big Questions.

Write About It!

Each article in your Student Anthology has an opportunity for you to Write About It! A writing assignment helps you think about the Big Question in a new way.

Draft It
A writing frame helps you organize your writing.

Writing Prompt
A prompt explains the assignment.

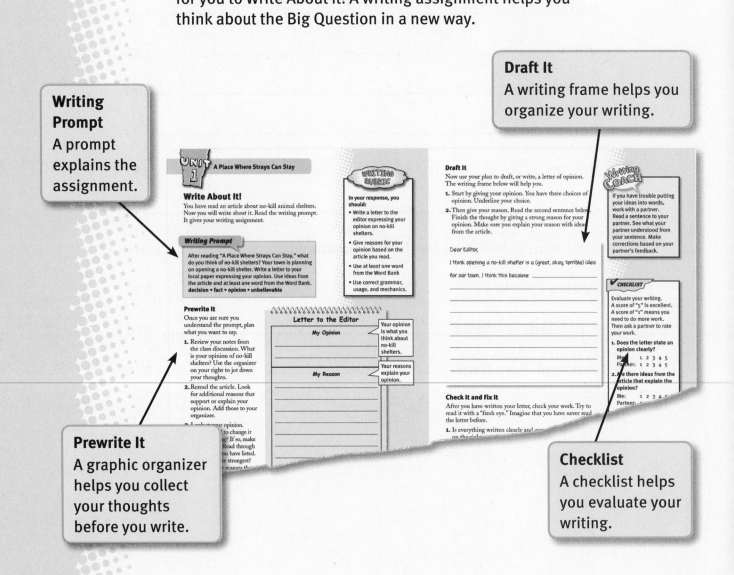

Prewrite It
A graphic organizer helps you collect your thoughts before you write.

Checklist
A checklist helps you evaluate your writing.

Vocabulary Workshop

Each article in your Student Anthology has a Vocabulary Workshop. In the workshop, you explore words from the Word Bank as you use them in different ways. Expanding your vocabulary will help you become a better reader and writer.

Your Choice
Record other words you want to remember.

Show You Know
Check your understanding about words by writing stories, crafting clues, or answering questions.

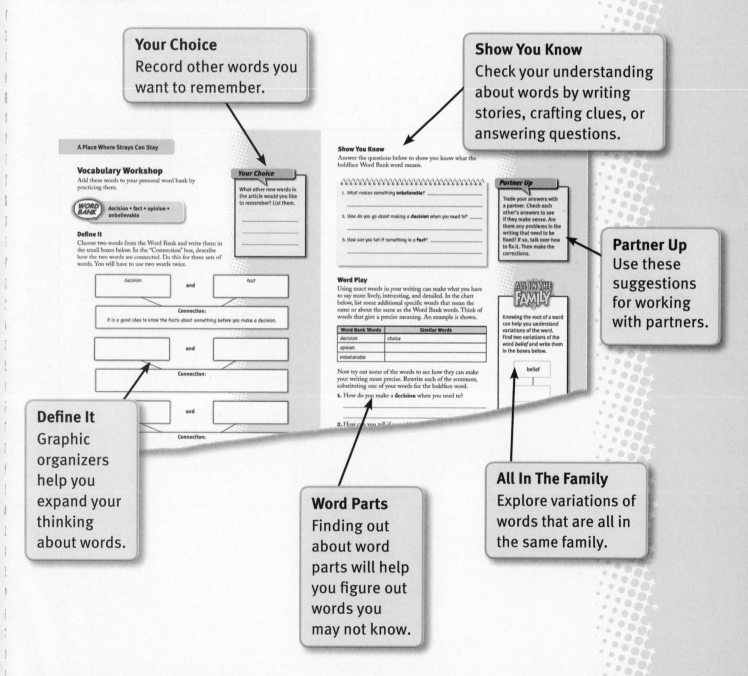

Define It
Graphic organizers help you expand your thinking about words.

Word Parts
Finding out about word parts will help you figure out words you may not know.

All In The Family
Explore variations of words that are all in the same family.

Partner Up
Use these suggestions for working with partners.

Grammar, Usage, and Mechanics Handbook

The Grammar, Usage, and Mechanics Handbook answers questions you may have during and after writing. It will help you correctly write and punctuate sentences. It will help you spell words that are commonly misspelled or confused.

Charts
Charts like this one help you find useful information about grammar, usage, and mechanics at a glance.

Writer's Alert
These alerts help you avoid common mistakes in your writing.

Exercise
As you practice grammar, usage, and mechanics, you will learn and remember strategies that will help your writing.

Nouns

A **noun** names a person, a place, or a thing.
Person: Mona is a student.
Place: My school is Marson Middle School.
Thing: That article is about baseball.

Regular Plurals
A **singular noun** names one person, place, or thing.
A **plural noun** names more than one person, place, or thing.
To form the plural of most nouns, add –s to the end of the noun.

Singular	Plural
one teenager	two teenagers
this computer	these computers
that government	those governments
a site	many sites

 A noncount noun, which names something you cannot count, does not have a plural form. Some common noncount nouns are *clothing, equipment, furniture, information, knowledge,* and *water.*

Exercise: Regular Plurals
Highlight and fix the five mistakes in noun plurals.

(1) There are several way to build knowledge about a subject.
(2) For example, you can look in an encyclopedia. (3) This helpful book has informations about many subject. (4) It will give you a factual explanation of each subject. (5) Most schools also have computer. (6) Student can use the Internet to search for useful facts.

Nouns continued

Special Noun Plurals
To make some nouns plural, you need to do more than add an –s ending. Use the chart to figure out how to spell these plurals.

Singular Noun Ending	Singular	Plural
When a noun ends in *ch, s, sh, x,* or *z,* add –es.	a lunch one dress that dish this box each waltz	two lunches many dresses those dishes these boxes several waltzes
When a noun ends in a consonant + *y,* change the *y* to *i* and add –es.	a country one penny every city	many countries several pennies ten cities
When a noun ends in *f* or *fe,* change the *f* to *v* and add –s or –es. Note: There are exceptions to this rule.	this leaf one knife a chief one roof	these leaves two knives several chiefs many roofs
When a noun ends in a consonant + *o,* add –es. Note: There are exceptions to this rule.	that hero a potato one piano an auto	those heroes a dozen potatoes many pianos several autos

 Do not use an apostrophe to form the plural of a noun.
Wrong: many belief's   **Right:** many beliefs

Exercise: Special Noun Plurals
Highlight and fix the misspelled plural in each sentence. Use the chart or a dictionary for help.

How do we decide what is true?

WRITING RUBRIC

Write About It!

You have read an article about no-kill animal shelters. Now you will write about it. Read the writing prompt. It gives your writing assignment.

Writing Prompt

After reading "A Place Where Strays Can Stay," what do you think of no-kill shelters? Your town is planning on opening a no-kill shelter. Write a letter to your local paper expressing your opinion. Use ideas from the article and at least one word from the Word Bank.
decision • fact • opinion • unbelievable

In your response, you should:

- Write a letter to the editor expressing your opinion on no-kill shelters.

- Give reasons for your opinion based on the article you read.

- Use at least one word from the Word Bank

- Use correct grammar, usage, and mechanics.

Prewrite It

Once you are sure you understand the prompt, plan what you want to say.

1. Review your notes from the class discussion. What is your opinion of no-kill shelters? Use the organizer on your right to jot down your thoughts.

2. Reread the article. Look for additional reasons that support or explain your opinion. Add those to your organizer.

3. Look at your opinion. Do you need to change it after rereading? If so, make the changes. Read through the reasons you have listed. Which are the strongest? Cross out the reasons that are not as strong.

Letter to the Editor

My Opinion

_____

_____

_____

Your opinion is what you think about no-kill shelters.

My Reason

_____

_____

_____

_____

_____

_____

_____

Your reasons explain your opinion.

Draft It

Now use your plan to draft, or write, a letter of opinion. The writing frame below will help you.

1. Start by giving your opinion. You have three choices of opinion. Underline your choice.

2. Then give your reason. Read the second sentence below. Finish the thought by giving a strong reason for your opinion. Make sure you explain your reason with ideas from the article.

Dear Editor,

I think opening a no-kill shelter is a (great, okay, terrible) idea

for our town. I think this because _____

_____

_____

_____

_____

_____

_____

_____

Check It and Fix It

After you have written your letter, check your work. Try to read it with a "fresh eye." Imagine that you have never read the letter before.

1. Is everything written clearly and correctly? Use the checklist on the right to see.

2. Trade your work with a classmate. Talk over ways you both might improve your letters. Use the ideas to revise your work.

3. For help with grammar, usage, and mechanics, go to the Handbook on pages 189–226.

If you have trouble putting your ideas into words, work with a partner. Read a sentence to your partner. See what your partner understood from your sentence. Make corrections based on your partner's feedback.

✔ CHECKLIST

Evaluate your writing. A score of "5" is excellent. A score of "1" means you need to do more work. Then ask a partner to rate your work.

1. **Does the letter state an opinion clearly?**

   Me: 1 2 3 4 5
   Partner: 1 2 3 4 5

2. **Are there ideas from the article that explain the opinion?**

   Me: 1 2 3 4 5
   Partner: 1 2 3 4 5

3. **Is there at least one Word Bank word used?**

   Me: 1 2 3 4 5
   Partner: 1 2 3 4 5

4. **Are grammar, usage, and mechanics correct?**

   Me: 1 2 3 4 5
   Partner: 1 2 3 4 5

Vocabulary Workshop

Add these words to your personal word bank by practicing them.

 **WORD BANK** decision • fact • opinion • unbelievable

Your Choice

What other new words in the article would you like to remember? List them.

_____

_____

_____

Define It

Choose two words from the Word Bank and write them in the small boxes below. In the "Connection" box, describe how the two words are connected. Do this for three sets of words. You will have to use two words twice.

decision	**and**	fact

Connection:
It is a good idea to know the facts about something before you make a decision.

	and	

Connection:

	and	

Connection:

Show You Know

Answer the questions below to show you know what the boldface Word Bank word means.

1. What makes something **unbelievable**? _____

_____

2. How do you go about making a **decision** when you need to? _____

_____

3. How can you tell if something is a **fact**? _____

_____

Partner Up

Trade your answers with a partner. Check each other's answers to see if they make sense. Are there any problems in the writing that need to be fixed? If so, talk over how to fix them. Then make the corrections.

Word Play

Using exact words in your writing can make what you have to say more lively, interesting, and detailed. In the chart below, list some additional specific words that mean the same or about the same as the Word Bank words. Think of words that give a precise meaning. An example is shown.

Word Bank Words	Similar Words
decision	choice
opinion	
unbelievable	

Now try out some of the words to see how they can make your writing more precise. Rewrite each of the sentences, substituting one of your words for the boldface word.

1. How do you make a **decision** when you need to?

_____

_____

2. How can you tell if something is an **opinion**? _____

3. What makes something **unbelievable**? _____

ALL IN THE FAMILY

Knowing the root of a word can help you understand variations of the word. Find two variations of the word *belief* and write them in the boxes below.

belief

_____

_____

A Place Where Strays Can Stay   **5**

Write About It!

You have read an article about peer pressure. Now you will write about it. Read the writing prompt. It gives your writing assignment.

Writing Prompt

After reading "Having Friends, Making Choices," how would you handle peer pressure? Write an advice column for your school newspaper about peer pressure and how to deal with it. Use ideas from the article and at least one word from the Word Bank.

notice • prove • study • test • true

In your response, you should:

- Write an advice column about peer pressure for your school newspaper.
- Give reasons for your advice based on the article you read.
- Use at least one word from the Word Bank.
- Use correct grammar, usage, and mechanics.

Prewrite It

Once you are sure you understand the prompt, plan what you want to say.

1. Review your notes from the class discussion. What advice would you give about handling peer pressure? Jot down your ideas in the organizer.

2. Reread the article. Look for additional reasons that support your advice. Add them to your organizer.

3. Look at your advice. Do you need to change it after rereading the article? If so, make the changes. Read through the organizer. Which are the best ideas to support your advice? Cross out the reasons that are not as strong.

Advice Column

My Advice

> Your advice is how you think people should handle peer pressure.

Strategies

> Your strategies explain how to do what you advise.

Draft It

Now use your plan to draft, or write, an advice column. The writing frame below will help you.

1. Start by writing down your advice. You have three choices of advice. Underline your choice.

2. Then give your strategies. Read the second sentence below. Finish it by giving a strong reason for your advice. Make sure you explain your reasons with ideas from the article.

If you have trouble putting your ideas into words, work with a partner. Explain to your partner what you want to say. Have your partner repeat your idea back to you in his or her own words. Then write down the idea based on what you both said.

THIS JUST IN

How to Handle Peer Pressure

The most effective way to handle peer pressure is to

(always say no, always say yes, trust your instincts). You

can handle pressure from friends if you _____

_____

_____

_____

_____

_____

_____

_____

✔ **CHECKLIST**

Evaluate your writing. A score of "5" is excellent. A score of "1" means you need to do more work. Then ask a partner to rate your work.

1. Does the column present advice clearly?

Me: 1 2 3 4 5
Partner: 1 2 3 4 5

2. Are there ideas from the article that support the advice?

Me: 1 2 3 4 5
Partner: 1 2 3 4 5

3. Is there at least one Word Bank word used?

Me: 1 2 3 4 5
Partner: 1 2 3 4 5

4. Are grammar, usage, and mechanics correct?

Me: 1 2 3 4 5
Partner: 1 2 3 4 5

Check It and Fix It

After you have written your advice column, check your work. Read it as if you are looking for advice on handling peer pressure. Does your advice make sense?

1. Is everything written clearly and correctly? Use the checklist on the right to see.

2. Exchange work with a classmate. Talk over ways to improve your advice columns. Use the ideas to revise your work.

3. For help with grammar, usage, and mechanics, go to the Handbook on pages 189–226.

Vocabulary Workshop

Add these words to your personal word bank by practicing them.

WORD BANK notice • prove • study • test • true

Define It

Choose two words from the Word Bank and write them on either side of the triangle below. Then describe how the two words are connected by completing the "because" portion of the sentence. Do this for three sets of words. You will have to use one word twice.

notice   **is connected to**   prove

because you must notice the facts about

something in order to prove it is true.

is connected to

because _____

_____

is connected to

because _____

_____

What other new words in the article would you like to remember? List them.

_____

_____

_____

The best way to remember new words is to use them soon after learning about them. Try to use one of your new words the next time you talk to someone. Use new words in and out of class.

Show You Know

Write a comic strip in the space below using all of the Word Bank words in a way that shows you understand their meanings.

Word Sort

Sort the Word Bank words by category, using the boxes below. Some words can be nouns and verbs, depending on how you use them in a sentence. Read through the article and find additional words you can add to each box. An example is shown.

Nouns	Verbs	Adjectives
	notice	

Now that you have sorted your words, pick two from different categories and combine them into a sentence. For a challenge, pick more than two to use in a sentence.

1. _____

   _____

2. _____

Knowing the root of a word can help you understand variations of the word. Find two variations of the root word *true* and write them in the boxes below.

```
  ┌──────────┐
  │   true   │
  └────┬─────┘
       │
  ┌────┴─────┐
  │          │
  └────┬─────┘
       │
  ┌────┴─────┐
  │          │
  └──────────┘
```

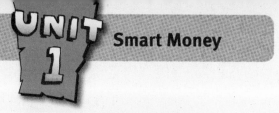

Write About It!

You have read an article about allowances. Now you will write about it. Read the writing prompt. It gives your writing assignment.

Writing Prompt

After reading "Smart Money," what is your opinion of allowances? Write a dialogue for a scene that has you and a friend debating two different points of view on allowances. Use ideas from the article and at least one word from the Word Bank.

confirm • determine • intently • opinion • realistic

WRITING RUBRIC

In your response, you should:

- Write a dialogue debating two different opinions of allowances.

- Give reasons for both opinions based on the article you read.

- Use at least one word from the Word Bank.

- Use correct grammar, usage, and mechanics.

Prewrite It

Once you are sure you understand the prompt, plan what you want to say.

1. Review your notes from the class discussion. What two opinions on allowances do you want to write about? Jot down your own opinion and a different opinion in the organizer.

2. Reread the article. Look for additional reasons that support both opinions. Add those to your organizer.

3. Look at the opinions you wrote down. Do you need to change them after rereading? If so, make the changes. Read through all the reasons you have listed. Cross out the reasons that are not as strong.

Allowance Debate

My Opinion	Friend's Opinion

Opinions are what people think about a subject.

My Reasons	Friend's Reasons

Reasons explain or support the opinions.

Draft It

Now use your plan to draft, or write, a dialogue. The writing frame below will help you.

1. Start by stating both opinions in dialogue form. State your opinions for each speaker by underlining your choices.

2. Then give your reasons. Read the sentences below. Finish the thoughts by giving strong reasons for each opinion. Be sure to explain the reasons with ideas from the article.

Me: I think kids (should, should not) get an allowance.

Friend: Well I think kids (should, should not) get an allowance.

M: I think this because _____

_____

_____

_____

F: I hear you, but I think the opposite because _____

_____

_____

_____

_____

Check It and Fix It

After you have written your dialogue, check your work. Read it to see if it sounds natural. Imagine you have not read it before.

1. Is everything written clearly and correctly? Use the checklist on the right to see.

2. Trade your work with a classmate. Talk over ways you both might improve your dialogues. Use the ideas to revise your work.

3. For help with grammar, usage, and mechanics, go to the Handbook on pages 189–226.

If you have trouble writing like someone would speak, work with a partner. Write down an idea and have your partner put it in his or her own words. Make corrections based on your partner's feedback.

✔ CHECKLIST

Evaluate your writing. A score of "5" is excellent. A score of "1" means you need to do more work. Then ask a partner to rate your work.

1. Does the dialogue state two opinions clearly?

Me: 1 2 3 4 5
Partner: 1 2 3 4 5

2. Are there ideas from the article that explain both opinions?

Me: 1 2 3 4 5
Partner: 1 2 3 4 5

3. Is there at least one Word Bank word used?

Me: 1 2 3 4 5
Partner: 1 2 3 4 5

4. Are grammar, usage, and mechanics correct?

Me: 1 2 3 4 5
Partner: 1 2 3 4 5

Vocabulary Workshop

Add these words to your personal word bank by practicing them.

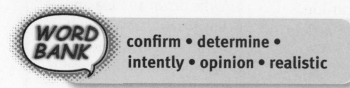

WORD BANK confirm • determine • intently • opinion • realistic

Define It

Complete the chart below. First, tell what each Word Bank word means. Then write the context clues from the article that help you understand the word's meaning. Remember that context clues are words or phrases around the word you do not know. The context words can give you clues to the difficult word's meaning.

Word	Meaning	Context Clues
confirm	to make sure something is true	A trip to the mall helps you confirm what people want.

Word COACH

When looking for context clues, certain key words can help you to understand the word you do not know. Words like *is, was, or, such as,* and *means* often point you to the meaning of the word you are having trouble with. For example, in the sentence, "One way to classify, or group, different kinds of cars is by engine," the word *or* points you to a definition of *classify*.

Show You Know

For each word from the Word Bank, write a clue sentence for a partner to see if he or she can match it with the correct term. See the example below for the word *opinion*.

- If you feel strongly about something, you probably have this.

1. _____

_____

2. _____

_____

3. _____

_____

4. _____

_____

Partner Up

To check your work, first trade clue sentences with a different partner. Make changes based on his or her feedback.

Word Endings: *-ion*

- When you add the word ending *-ion* to a verb, you change the word from an action into a thing (a noun).

  Verb: Please **confirm** that you will be attending the party.

  Noun: We received your **confirmation** that you will be at the party.

- Circle the correct form of the words in parentheses.

  It was the school's (determine, determination) that our debate team would skip the regional contest. I know the school's (intention, intent, intently) is to make a statement, but I think the team should (determination, determine) whether they go or not. We were not sure about the whole situation until the debate coach provided (confirm, confirmation, confirming) of the school's decision last night.

ALL IN THE FAMILY

Knowing the root of a word can help you understand variations of the word. Find two variations of the root word *real* and write them in the boxes below. They can be from the article you read or you can look them up in a dictionary.

real

Write About It!

You have read an article about community policing. Now you will write about it. Read the writing prompt. It gives your writing assignment.

Writing Prompt

After reading "Policing Changes," what characteristics do you think would be best for a community police officer? Write a job description for a police officer position in your community. Use ideas from the article and at least one word from the Word Bank.

decision • depend • evidence • examine • investigate

WRITING RUBRIC

In your response, you should:

- Write a job description for a community policing position.

- Provide details based on the article you read.

- Use at least one word from the Word Bank.

- Use correct grammar, usage, and mechanics.

Prewrite It

Once you are sure you understand the prompt, plan what you want to say.

1. Review your notes from the class discussion. What characteristics would you like to see in a community police officer? Use the organizer to make notes. Be sure to explain why each characteristic is important.

2. Reread the article. Look for additional ideas to create your job description. Add those to your organizer.

3. Look at your notes. Are there characteristics you have written down that go together? If so, lump them together to organize your thoughts. Cross out ideas that are not as strong.

Community Police Officer Job

Characteristic and Explanation 1

Characteristic and Explanation 2

Characteristic and Explanation 3

Characteristics describe a person's personality and attitude.

Draft It

Now use your plan to draft, or write, a job description. The writing frame below will help you.

1. Start by describing the type of person you want to fill the job. You have three choices. Underline your choice.

2. Then give details about the characteristics you are looking for in a community officer. Read the second sentence below and finish the thought. Make sure you include ideas from the article in the job description.

THIS JUST IN

Community Police Officer Needed

We are a looking for a (friendly, serious, committed)

community police officer. Our neighborhood wants an

officer who _____

_____

_____

_____

_____

_____

_____

Work with a partner if you are having trouble writing out your ideas. Read a sentence to your partner. See what your partner understood from your sentence. Make corrections based on your partner's feedback.

✔ **CHECKLIST**

Evaluate your writing. A score of "5" is excellent. A score of "1" means you need to do more work. Then ask a partner to rate your work.

1. **Does the job description clearly present the desired characteristics?**

   Me: 1 2 3 4 5
   Partner: 1 2 3 4 5

2. **Are there ideas from the article that describe the desired characteristics?**

   Me: 1 2 3 4 5
   Partner: 1 2 3 4 5

3. **Is there at least one Word Bank word used?**

   Me: 1 2 3 4 5
   Partner: 1 2 3 4 5

4. **Are grammar, usage, and mechanics correct ?**

   Me: 1 2 3 4 5
   Partner: 1 2 3 4 5

Check It and Fix It

After you have written your job description, check your work. Imagine that you have never heard about community police officers. Make sure that the information is accurate.

1. Is everything written clearly and correctly? Use the checklist on the right to see.

2. Exchange work with a classmate. Talk over ways to improve your job descriptions. Use the ideas to revise your work.

3. For help with grammar, usage, and mechanics, go to the Handbook on pages 189–226.

Vocabulary Workshop

Add these words to your personal word bank by practicing them.

 **WORD BANK** decision • depend • evidence • examine • investigate

Your Choice

What other new words in the article would you like to remember? List them.

_____

_____

_____

Define It

Choose two words from the Word Bank and write them in the Venn diagram circles below. Where the circles intersect, describe how the two words could be connected. Do this for three sets of words. You will have to use one word twice.

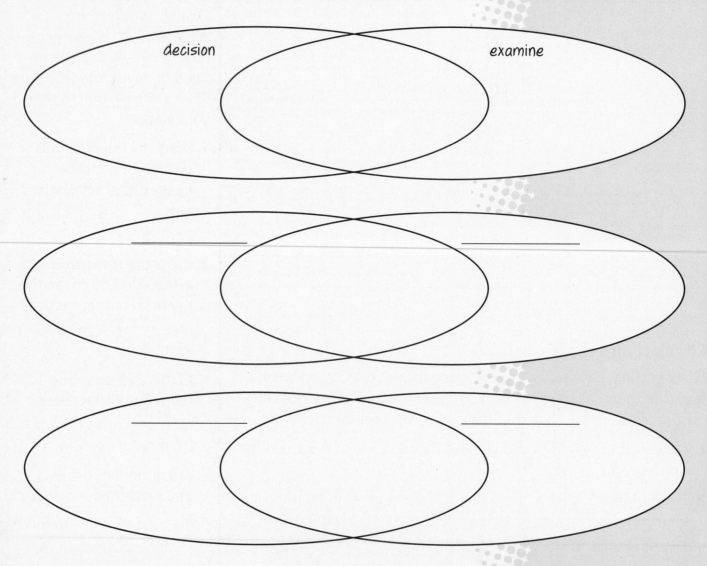

decision   examine

Show You Know

Write a short, short story (just one paragraph!) using the Word Bank words in the space below. Be sure your sentences show that you understand the meanings of the words. You can use Word Bank words more than once, but make sure you use them all at least once. The sentence below should get you started.

You can imagine my surprise when _____

_____

_____

_____

_____

Partner Up

After you write your short, short story, trade stories with a partner. Check each other's writing to see if the story makes sense. Are there any problems in the writing that need to be fixed? If so, talk over how to fix them. Then make the corrections.

Word Play

Using exact words in your writing can make what you say more lively, interesting, and detailed. In the chart below, list some additional specific words that mean the same or about the same as the Word Bank words. Think of words that give a precise meaning. Examples are shown.

Word Bank Words	Similar Words
depend	rely, count on
evidence	
investigate	

Now try out some of the words to see how they can make writing more precise. Rewrite each of the sentences, substituting one of your words for the boldface word.

1. I need **evidence** before I can really know what happened.

_____

_____

2. Can I **depend** on you to **investigate** this matter?

_____

_____

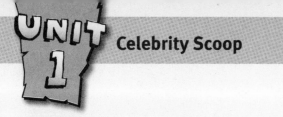

Write About It!

You have read an article about celebrities and their right to privacy. Now you will write about it. Read the writing prompt. It gives your writing assignment.

Writing Prompt

After reading "Celebrity Scoop," imagine you are a TV executive. Write a memo to the news staff about covering more or less celebrity news. Use ideas from the article and at least one word from the Word Bank.

consequence • determine • prove • true • unbelievable

WRITING RUBRIC

In your response, you should:

- Write a memo explaining why the station will be covering more or less celebrity news.

- Give reasons for your decision based on the article you read.

- Use at least one word from the Word Bank.

- Use correct grammar, usage, and mechanics.

Prewrite It

Once you are sure you understand the prompt, plan what you want to say.

1. Review your notes from the class discussion. Will your station cover more or less celebrity news? Jot down your decision in the organizer.

2. Reread the article. Look for additional reasons that support or explain your decision. Add those to your organizer.

3. Look at your decision. Do you need to change it after rereading the article? If so, make the changes. Read through all the reasons you have listed. Cross out the reasons that are not as strong.

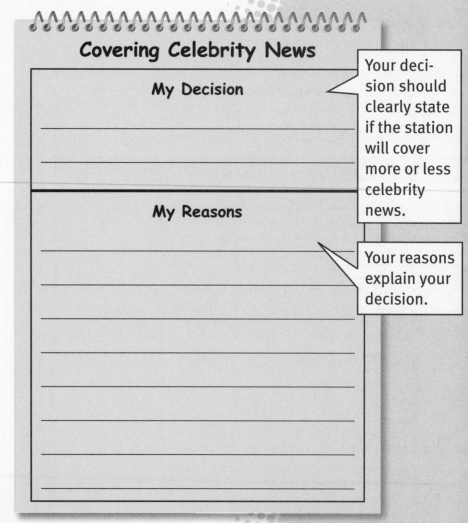

Covering Celebrity News

My Decision

Your decision should clearly state if the station will cover more or less celebrity news.

My Reasons

Your reasons explain your decision.

Draft It

Now use your plan to draft, or write, a memo. The writing frame below will help you.

1. Start by stating your decision. You have two choices. Underline your decision.

2. Then give your reasons. Read the second sentence below. Finish it by giving a strong reason for your decision. Be sure to explain your reasons with ideas from the article.

Staff Memo

Re: Celebrity News Coverage

After much thought, I have decided that our station will cover (more, less) celebrity news. This is because _____

_____

_____

_____

_____

_____

_____

Check It and Fix It

After you have written your memo, check your work. Read it with a "fresh eye," looking for clear support for an opinion about celebrity news coverage.

1. Is everything written clearly and correctly? Use the checklist on the right to see.

2. Trade your work with a classmate. Talk over ways to improve your memos. Use the ideas to revise your work.

3. For help with grammar, usage, and mechanics, go to the Handbook on pages 189–226.

✔ CHECKLIST

Evaluate your writing. A score of "5" is excellent. A score of "1" means you need to do more work. Then ask a partner to rate your work.

1. **Does the memo clearly state a decision?**
   Me: 1 2 3 4 5
   Partner: 1 2 3 4 5

2. **Are there ideas from the article that help explain the decision?**
   Me: 1 2 3 4 5
   Partner: 1 2 3 4 5

3. **Is there at least one Word Bank word used?**
   Me: 1 2 3 4 5
   Partner: 1 2 3 4 5

4. **Are grammar, usage, and mechanics correct?**
   Me: 1 2 3 4 5
   Partner: 1 2 3 4 5

Vocabulary Workshop

Add these words to your personal word bank by practicing them.

consequence • determine • prove • true • unbelievable

Your Choice

What other new words in the article would you like to remember? List them.

_____

_____

_____

Define It

Choose two words from the Word Bank and write them in the small boxes below. In the "Connection" box, describe how the two words are connected. Do this for three sets of words. You will have to use one word twice.

determine

and

consequence

Connection:

and

Connection:

and

Connection:

Show You Know

Answer the questions below to show you know what each boldface Word Bank word means.

1. If you have to deal with the **consequence** of an action, what does that mean? _____

_____

2. How would you **prove** something to someone who did not believe you? _____

_____

3. How might you **determine** the winner of a really close race? _____

_____

4. Which is easier to **believe**: that UFOs exist, or that panthers exist? Why? _____

_____

Word Beginnings: *dis-*, *un-*

- When you add prefixes to words, you change their meanings.

    dis-: not, away from, or apart

    un-: not, the opposite of

- Use the prefixes to change the meanings of these words from the article:

    dis-: prove

    un-: true, determined

- Circle the correct word in parentheses.

    A scientist will try to (prove, disprove) a new theory and show it is wrong in order to test the theory. This is called peer review, and scientists depend on it to (undetermined, determine) whether a new theory is really worthwhile or not. If they find the theory has problems or is (untrue, true), more research will need to be done to come up with a newer theory.

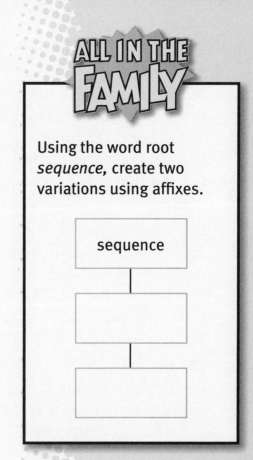

ALL IN THE FAMILY

Using the word root *sequence,* create two variations using affixes.

sequence

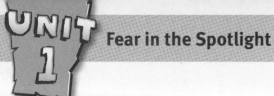

Write About It!

You have read an article about stage fright. Now you will write about it. Read the writing prompt. It gives your writing assignment.

WRITING RUBRIC

In your response, you should:

- Write a paragraph about a personal experience with fear and how you dealt with it.

- Use ideas from the article you read to explain your fear and reaction to it.

- Use at least one word from the Word Bank.

- Use correct grammar, usage, and mechanics.

Writing Prompt

After reading "Fear in the Spotlight," did it remind you of any experiences you've had with stage fright? Write a paragraph about a personal experience with fear and how you dealt with it. Use ideas from the article and at least one word from the Word Bank.

audience • confirm • fact • fantasy • fiction

Prewrite It

Once you are sure you understand the prompt, plan what you want to say.

1. Review your notes from the class discussion. Think about an event in your life that caused you to feel fear. Jot down notes in the organizer.

2. Reread the article. Look for additional ideas to explain your personal experience. Add those to your organizer.

3. Look at your organizer. Do any of your descriptions need to be changed after rereading the article? Do you need more details? If so, make the changes or additions.

My Fear Experience

What Frightened Me

Here you should describe what happened.

How I Felt	How I Responded

These sections should include specific details about your experience.

Draft It

Now use your plan to draft, or write, a paragraph. The writing frame below will help you.

1. Start by describing your own fearful experience. Use the first sentence below as a way to get started.

2. Then give details about how you felt and how you responded to the situation. Make sure you use ideas from the article to explain your experience.

I had a fearful experience when _____

_____

_____

At the beginning, I felt _____

_____

_____

_____

_____

Then I _____

_____

_____

_____

Check It and Fix It

After you have written your paragraph, check your work. Check to be sure that the paragraph describes both an experience and how you reacted to it.

1. Is everything written clearly and correctly? Use the checklist on the right to see.

2. Exchange your work with a classmate and talk over ways you both might improve the descriptions in your paragraphs. Use the ideas to revise your work.

3. For help with grammar, usage, and mechanics, go to the Handbook on pages 189–226.

Writing COACH

Work with a partner to test your descriptions. Read what you have written and ask your partner if he or she can "see" what you are describing. Make changes based on the feedback from your partner.

✔ **CHECKLIST**

Evaluate your writing. A score of "5" is excellent. A score of "1" means you need to do more work. Then ask a partner to rate your work.

1. Does the paragraph clearly explain the experience?

Me: 1 2 3 4 5
Partner: 1 2 3 4 5

2. Are there ideas from the article that help the description?

Me: 1 2 3 4 5
Partner: 1 2 3 4 5

3. Is there at least one Word Bank word used?

Me: 1 2 3 4 5
Partner: 1 2 3 4 5

4. Are grammar, usage, and mechanics correct?

Me: 1 2 3 4 5
Partner: 1 2 3 4 5

Vocabulary Workshop

Add these words to your personal word bank by practicing them.

 audience • confirm • fact • fantasy • fiction

Define It

Complete the chart below. First, tell what the Word Bank word means. Then tell what the word does not mean. Use the example as a guide.

Word	What It Is	What It Is Not
fiction	something that is made up	something you can prove

An antonym is a word that means the opposite. For example, *hot* is an antonym for *cold*. It is sometimes helpful to describe something by what it is not. Try to describe a room to a friend only using antonyms.

Show You Know

To show that you understand the Word Bank words, write three sentences. In each sentence, use and highlight two of the Word Bank words. You will use one word twice. Use the example as a model.

- Fantasy writers never let facts get in the way of the story.

1. _____

_____

2. _____

_____

3. _____

_____

Word Sort

Sort the Word Bank words by category, using the boxes below. Read through the article and find additional words you can add to each box. Examples are shown.

Nouns	Verbs	Adjectives
audience		factual

Now that you have sorted your words, pick two from different categories and combine them into a sentence. For a challenge, pick more than two to use in a sentence.

1. _____

_____

2. _____

_____

Write About It!

You have read an article about how you get to know someone. Now you will write about it. Read the writing prompt. It gives your writing assignment.

Writing Prompt

After reading "Facebook or Face-to-Face?" do you think you can safely meet others online? Create a flyer about Internet safety. Start with an introduction, then write a list of Do's and Don'ts. Use ideas from the article and at least one word from the Word Bank.
argue • constant • fiction • investigate • opinion

In your response, you should:

- Write a short introduction and a list of do's and don'ts for meeting people online.

- Use specific ideas from the article to create your flyer.

- Use at least one word from the Word Bank.

- Use correct grammar, usage, and mechanics.

Prewrite It

Once you are sure you understand the prompt, plan what you want to say.

1. Review your notes from the class discussion. Think of an introduction to your Do's and Don'ts list. Jot down other ideas and notes in the organizer.

2. Reread the article. Look for additional ideas that might help you write. Add those to your organizer.

3. Look at your organizer. Does your introduction need to be changed after rereading the article? If so, make the changes or additions. Read through your Do's and Don'ts. Cross out the notes that are least important.

Internet Safety Flyer

Introduction

Your introduction should let people know the purpose for your Do's and Don'ts list.

Do's	Don'ts

These sections should include specific advice from the article.

Draft It

Now use your plan to draft, or write, the flyer. The writing frame below will help you.

1. Start by introducing the purpose for your Do's and Don'ts list. Use the first sentence to help you get started.

2. Then create your Do's and Don'ts list. Make sure you use ideas from the article.

Work with a partner to make sure your Do's and Don'ts lists are not leaving out something important. Have your partner tell you what his or her Do's and Don'ts would be. Compare them to your list.

Internet Safety Flyer

The Internet is great, but if you are going to use it to

meet people, _____

_____

Internet Do's	Internet Don'ts
•	•
•	•
•	•

Check It and Fix It

After you have written your flyer, check your work. As you read, imagine that you do not know anything about Internet safety. Be sure your list makes sense.

1. Is everything written clearly and correctly? Use the checklist on the right to see.

2. Exchange your work with a classmate and talk over ways you both might improve the descriptions in your flyers. Use the ideas to revise your work.

3. For help with grammar, usage, and mechanics, go to the Handbook on pages 189–226.

✔ **CHECKLIST**

Evaluate your writing. A score of "5" is excellent. A score of "1" means you need to do more work. Then ask a partner to rate your work.

1. **Does the introduction clearly explain the purpose of the list?**

   Me: 1 2 3 4 5
   Partner: 1 2 3 4 5

2. **Are there ideas from the article in the list?**

   Me: 1 2 3 4 5
   Partner: 1 2 3 4 5

3. **Is there at least one Word Bank word used?**

   Me: 1 2 3 4 5
   Partner: 1 2 3 4 5

4. **Are grammar, usage, and mechanics correct?**

   Me: 1 2 3 4 5
   Partner: 1 2 3 4 5

Vocabulary Workshop

Add these words to your personal word bank by practicing them.

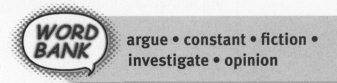

WORD BANK argue • constant • fiction • investigate • opinion

Your Choice

What other new words in the article would you like to remember? List them.

_____

_____

_____

Define It

Complete the chart below. First, tell what the Word Bank word means. Then describe your connection to the word. It can be a memory, or it can be what the word makes you think of when you read or hear it. Use the example as a guide.

Word	What It Is	My Connection
argue	when you and another person are talking and do not agree	my older sister, because she and I argue about everything

Show You Know

For three words from the Word Bank, write a clue sentence for a partner to see if he or she can match it with the correct word. See the example below for the word *investigate*.

- If you are a reporter working on a story about a mysterious disappearance, you are going to need to do this.

1. _____

   _____

2. _____

   _____

3. _____

   _____

Partner Up

After you write your clue sentences, trade them with a partner. Check each other's answers to make sure you both got them right. Then try to come up with a couple of extras using variations of the Word Bank words found in the article. For example, use *argument* or *constantly* in a clue sentence.

Word Sort

Sort the Word Bank words by category, using the boxes below. Read through the article and find additional words you can add to each box. An example is shown.

Nouns	Verbs	Adjectives
fiction		

Now that you have sorted your words, pick two from different categories and combine them into a sentence. For a challenge, use more than two in a sentence.

1. _____

   _____

2. _____

   _____

UNIT 1

The Fear Factor

Write About It!

You have read an article about phobias. Now you will write about it. Read the writing prompt. It gives your writing assignment.

Writing Prompt

After reading "The Fear Factor," do you think phobias are real or just all in our heads? Write a summary of the article for a Web site that is targeted to fifth graders. Use ideas from the article and at least one word from the Word Bank.

evidence • quote • realistic • study • test

In your response, you should:

- Write a summary of the phobia article for a Web site that is targeted to fifth graders.

- Use specific ideas from the article to create your summary.

- Use at least one word from the Word Bank.

- Use correct grammar, usage, and mechanics.

Prewrite It

Once you are sure you understand the prompt, plan what you want to say.

1. Review your notes from the class discussion. Jot down your thoughts on the different types and causes of phobias in the organizer.

2. Reread the article. Look for additional ideas for your summary. Add those to your organizer.

3. Take another look at your organizer. Do any of your notes need to be changed after rereading the article? If so, make the changes or additions. Read through all of your notes. Cross out the notes that are not as important.

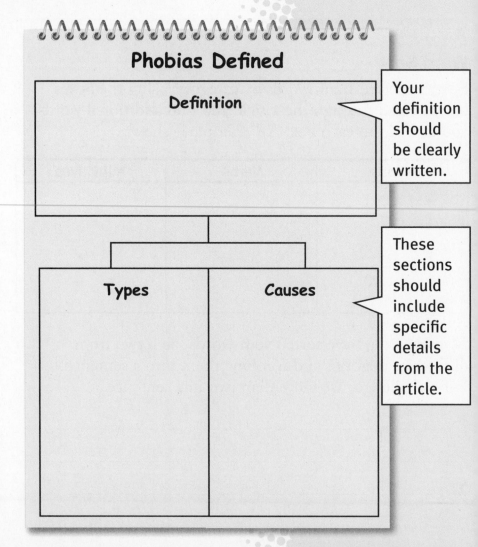

Phobias Defined

Definition

Your definition should be clearly written.

Types   Causes

These sections should include specific details from the article.

Draft It

Now use your plan to draft, or write, the summary.
The writing frame below will help you.

1. Start by defining what phobias are. Use the first sentence below as a way to get started.

2. Then give details about the types and causes of phobias. Make sure you use ideas from the article in the summary.

Phobias are different from fears because _____

_____

_____

Though there are many types of phobias, _____

_____

_____

_____

_____

_____

_____

_____

Check It and Fix It

After you have written your summary, check your work. Try to read it with a "fresh eye." Imagine that you do not know anything about phobias.

1. Is everything written clearly and correctly? Use the checklist on the right to see.

2. Exchange your work with a classmate and talk over ways you both might improve the descriptions in your summaries. Use the ideas to revise your work.

3. For help with grammar, usage, and mechanics, go to the Handbook on pages 189–226.

If you have trouble putting your ideas into words, work with a partner. Explain to your partner what you want to say. Have your partner repeat your idea back to you in his or her own words. Then write down the idea based on what you both said.

✔ CHECKLIST

Evaluate your writing. A score of "5" is excellent. A score of "1" means you need to do more work. Then ask a partner to rate your work.

1. Does the summary explain phobias clearly?

Me: 1 2 3 4 5
Partner: 1 2 3 4 5

2. Are there ideas from the article that help describe phobias?

Me: 1 2 3 4 5
Partner: 1 2 3 4 5

3. Is there at least one Word Bank word used?

Me: 1 2 3 4 5
Partner: 1 2 3 4 5

4. Are grammar, usage, and mechanics correct?

Me: 1 2 3 4 5
Partner: 1 2 3 4 5

Vocabulary Workshop

Add these words to your personal word bank by practicing them.

WORD BANK evidence • quote • realistic • study • test

Your Choice

What other new words in the article would you like to remember? List them.

_____

_____

_____

Define It

Choose two words from the Word Bank and write them on either side of the triangle below. Then describe how the two words are connected by completing the "because" portion of the sentence. Do this for three sets of words. You will have to use one word twice.

study **is connected to** evidence

because _____

_____

is connected to

because _____

_____

is connected to

because _____

_____

Show You Know

Write a comic strip in the space below using all of the Word Bank words in a way that shows you understand their meanings.

Word Play

Using exact words in your writing can make what you say more lively, interesting, and detailed. In the chart below, list some additional specific words that mean the same or about the same as the Word Bank words. Think of words that give a precise meaning. Examples are shown.

Word Bank Words	Similar Words
evidence	facts, proof, support
quote	
study	
test	

Now try out some of the words to see how they can make your writing more precise. Rewrite each of the sentences below, substituting one of your words for the boldface word.

1. Did you read the Coach's **quote** in the paper? _____

_____

2. I had to **study** like crazy for today's **test**. _____

_____

Writing Reflection

 How do we decide what is true?

Look through your writing from this unit and choose the best piece.
Reflect on this piece of writing by completing each sentence below.

My best piece of writing from this unit is _____

_____

I chose this piece because _____

_____

_____

While I was writing, one goal I had was _____

_____

I accomplished this goal by _____

_____

_____

This writing helped me think more about the Big Question because _____

_____

_____

One thing I learned while writing that can help me in the future is _____

_____

_____

 Is conflict always bad?

Write About It!

You have read an article about birth order in families. Now you will write about it. Read the writing prompt. It gives your writing assignment.

WRITING RUBRIC

In your response, you should:

• Write dialogue between two siblings.

• Use details about birth order from the article to support the dialogue.

• Use at least one word from the Word Bank.

• Use correct grammar, usage, and mechanics.

Writing Prompt

After reading "Does Birth Order Matter?" imagine that you are the writer for a reality-based soap opera. Write a dialogue between two siblings arguing over their role in the family. Use ideas from the article and at least one word from the Word Bank.

argue • compete • instructions • lose • negotiate

Prewrite It

Once you are sure you understand the prompt, plan what you want to say.

1. Review your notes from the class discussion. Jot down notes in the organizer.

2. Reread the article. Look for details about birth order characteristics.

3. You are writing a dialogue between two siblings. Decide if you are writing from the point of view of the youngest, middle, or the oldest. (You will need to pick two.) Cross out the part of the organizer that you are not going to use. In the other parts of the organizer, circle the characteristics that you think are most important.

Characteristics Based on Birth Order

Youngest	Middle	Oldest

Draft It

Now use your plan to draft, or write, your dialogue. The writing frame below will help you.

1. In dialogue, you first write each speaker's name, followed by a colon. Write the names on the lines before the colons.

2. Write the dialogue. Be sure that the dialogue sounds like real people talking and uses ideas about birth order. The youngest sibling, for example, might say, "Do not be jealous that I am more popular than you because I am younger!"

_____ : _____

_____

_____ : _____

_____

_____ : _____

_____

_____ : _____

_____

Check It and Fix It

After you have written your dialogue, check your work. You might read it aloud with a partner to see if it sounds natural.

1. Is everything written clearly and correctly? Use the checklist on the right to see.

2. Trade your work with a classmate. Talk over ways to improve your dialogues. Use the ideas to revise your work.

3. For help with grammar, usage, and mechanics, go to the Handbook on pages 189–226.

Writing COACH

If you have trouble with dialogue, think about the way that people talk. Make your dialogue sound natural. Listen to your friends in the hallway or at the lunch table. Then think about what you heard as you write.

✔ CHECKLIST

Evaluate your writing. A score of "5" is excellent. A score of "1" means you need to do more work. Then ask a partner to rate your work.

1. **Does the dialogue sound like real people talking?**

   Me: 1 2 3 4 5
   Partner: 1 2 3 4 5

2. **Do the siblings in the dialogue have the traits of the oldest, youngest, or middle sibling?**

   Me: 1 2 3 4 5
   Partner: 1 2 3 4 5

3. **Is there at least one Word Bank word used?**

   Me: 1 2 3 4 5
   Partner: 1 2 3 4 5

4. **Are grammar, usage, and mechanics correct?**

   Me: 1 2 3 4 5
   Partner: 1 2 3 4 5

Vocabulary Workshop

Add these words to your personal word bank by practicing them.

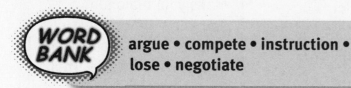

WORD BANK argue • compete • instruction • lose • negotiate

Your Choice

What other new words in the article would you like to remember? List them.

_____

_____

_____

Define It

Complete the chart below. First, give a real-life example of each Word Bank word. Then, write your connection to the word. Use the example as a guide.

Word	Real-Life Example	Connection
argue	an umpire and a player disagreeing over a call	I argue with my sister about chores.

Show You Know

To show that you understand the Word Bank words, write two sentences. In each sentence, use and highlight two of the Word Bank words. Use the example as a model.

- Lawyers argue cases and negotiate solutions.

1. _____

_____

2. _____

_____

Partner Up

Trade sentences with a partner. Check each other's sentences. If something needs fixing, talk over how to fix it. Then make the corrections.

Word Play

Using exact words in your writing can make what you have to say more lively, interesting, and detailed. In the chart below, list some more specific words that mean the same or about the same as the Word Bank words shown. Think of words that give a precise meaning. Examples are shown.

Word Bank Words	Similar Words
argue	bicker, quarrel
compete	
lose	

Now try out some of the words to see how they can make your writing more precise. Rewrite each of the sentences, substituting one of your words for the boldface word.

1. My sister and I **argue** over chores. _____

_____

2. The final teams will **compete** Friday. _____

_____

3. The crowd went quiet when the favored team **lost**.

_____

_____

Write About It!

You have read an article about steps for dealing with conflicts. Now you will write about it. Read the writing prompt. It gives your writing assignment.

Writing Prompt

After reading "Dealing with Conflicts," what do you think is the best way to handle conflicts? Imagine that you work at a peer mediation center in your neighborhood. Write a flyer that gives important information on peers and conflict. Use ideas from the article and at least one word from the Word Bank.

battle • defend • explain • negotiate • resolve

In your response, you should:

- Write an informational flyer about peers and conflict.

- Use details from the article in your writing.

- Use at least one word from the Word Bank.

- Use correct grammar, usage, and mechanics.

Prewrite It

Once you are sure you understand the prompt, plan what you want to say.

1. Review your notes from the class discussion. Jot down your thoughts on the concept web.

2. Reread the article. Look for additional details about peers and conflict. List them on the web.

3. You are writing an informational flyer for people who do not know about ways for peers to handle conflict. Circle the most important ideas on your web so that you will remember to use them. Cross out any ideas you do not want to include.

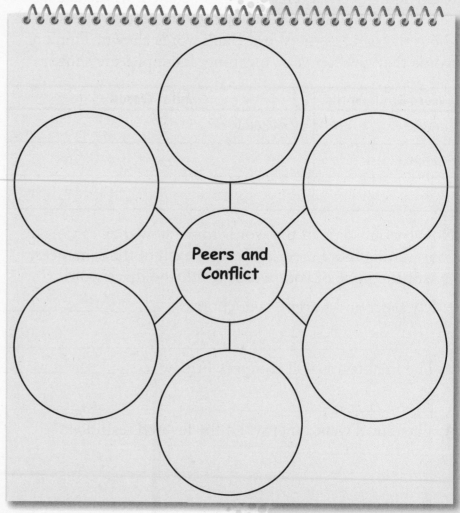

Draft It

Now use your plan to draft, or write, your flyer. The writing frame below will help you.

1. A flyer includes information. The people reading your flyer do not know about ways to handle conflict.

2. Use the writing frame to list the most important things your readers need to know about the new mediation center. You could tell what will happen at the mediation center, why people might want to go, and so on.

If you are having trouble writing the flyer, think about your audience. If your readers do not know anything about how peers handle conflict, what do they need to know?

Grand Opening!

Peer Mediation Center

Want to find out more? Here's what you need to know:

-
-
-
-

Check It and Fix It

After you have written your flyer, check your work. Imagine that you do not know anything about how to solve conflicts, and you are looking at this flyer to find out more.

1. Is everything written clearly and correctly? Use the checklist on the right to see.

2. Trade your work with a classmate. Talk over ways you both might improve flyers. Use the ideas to revise your work.

3. For help with grammar, usage, and mechanics, go to the Handbook on pages 189–226.

Vocabulary Workshop

Add these words to your personal word bank by practicing them.

 **battle • defend • explain • negotiate • resolve**

Define It

Complete the chart below. First, write what each Word Bank word means. Then tell what clues in the article help you figure out what the word means. Use the example as a guide.

Word	Meaning	Clues from Article
battle	a fight; a struggle	You do not want a battle, but someone might get mad at you. That means that a battle happens when someone is mad.

When you cannot figure out the meaning of a word, look at the context. Context clues are words that help you figure out a word you do not know. Look in the sentence that has the word, and at the sentences before and after the one with the word.

Show You Know

For each word from the Word Bank, write a clue sentence for a partner to see if he or she can match it with the correct term. See the example below for the word *battle*.

• You do this when you have an opponent in a game like chess.

1. _____

   _____

2. _____

   _____

3. _____

   _____

4. _____

   _____

Partner Up

Trade sentences with a partner. Check each other's sentences. If something needs fixing, talk over how to fix it. Then make the corrections.

Word Endings: *-ion*

• When you add the word ending *-ion* to a verb, you change the verb (an action) into a noun (a thing). Many verbs change their spelling when the ending is added.

Verb: Mr. Thompson will **explain** the math problem.
Noun: His **explanation** is easy to understand.
Verb: Can Kyra and Mel **resolve** their problem?
Noun: One **resolution** might be to take turns.

• Circle the right form of the word in parentheses.

When you and a friend disagree, it helps to (explain, explanation) your point of view. Sometimes, a simple (explain, explanation) will solve the problem. Some problems, though, are harder to (resolve, resolution). You might need help to come to a (resolve, resolution).

ALL IN THE FAMILY

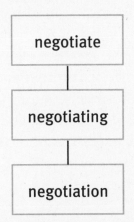

All these words are forms of *negotiate*. How does each ending change the meaning of the word?

negotiate
negotiating
negotiation

Write About It!

You have read an article about animal heroes and what might make these animals do such special things. Now you will write about it. Read the writing prompt. It gives your writing assignment.

Writing Prompt

After reading "Animal Heroes," suppose that you are a reporter for a local newspaper. Write an article that tells about an animal and its heroism. Use ideas from the article and at least one word from the Word Bank.

challenge • conclude • direction • lose • survival

WRITING RUBRIC

In your response, you should:

- Write a newspaper article about an animal hero.

- Use details from the article or from research.

- Use at least one word from the Word Bank.

- Use correct grammar, usage, and mechanics.

Prewrite It

Once you are sure you understand the prompt, plan what you want to say.

1. Review your notes from the class discussion. Begin to answer the questions in the table.

2. Reread the article. Look for additional details that you can add to the table.

3. You might want to write about an animal hero that you did not read about in the article. If so, use print or Internet sources to research an animal hero. Fill in the chart with details about the hero and what that hero accomplished.

An Animal Hero

Who is the hero?

What did the hero do?

When and where did this happen?

What else is important to know?

Draft It

Now use your plan to draft, or write, your newspaper article. The writing frame below will help you.

1. A newspaper article needs a hook for readers. Write an exciting short headline on the blank line below that will get readers wanting to read more.

2. A newspaper article tells important facts that answer the five *W* questions: *Who? What? When? Where?* and *Why?*

Your job in writing a newspaper article is to give facts. To see if a piece of information is a fact, ask, *Is this something I can prove is true?*

THIS JUST IN

_____

What makes an animal a hero? This story could answer

that question. _____

_____

_____

_____

_____

_____

_____

_____

_____

Check It and Fix It

After you have written your article, check your work. Read it as if you have never seen it before. See if you can find out the answers to *Who? What? When? Where?* and *Why?* as you read.

1. Is everything written clearly and correctly? Use the checklist on the right to see.

2. Trade your work with a classmate. Talk over ways to improve your articles. Use the ideas to revise your work.

3. For help with grammar, usage, and mechanics, go to the Handbook on pages 189–226.

✔ CHECKLIST

Evaluate your writing. A score of "5" is excellent. A score of "1" means you need to do more work. Then ask a partner to rate your work.

1. **Does the article answer the 5 Ws about an incident that has to do with an animal hero?**

   Me: 1 2 3 4 5
   Partner: 1 2 3 4 5

2. **Does the writing include information from the article or from reliable research?**

   Me: 1 2 3 4 5
   Partner: 1 2 3 4 5

3. **Is there at least one Word Bank word used?**

   Me: 1 2 3 4 5
   Partner: 1 2 3 4 5

4. **Are grammar, usage, and mechanics correct?**

   Me: 1 2 3 4 5
   Partner: 1 2 3 4 5

Vocabulary Workshop

Add these words to your personal word bank by practicing them.

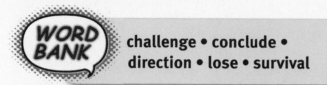

WORD BANK

challenge • conclude • direction • lose • survival

What other new words in the article would you like to remember? List them.

_____

_____

_____

Define It

Look at each pair of words. Explain how the two Word Bank words might be connected. For example, how could *challenge* and *survival* be connected? *Survival* in a difficult situation could be a *challenge*.

challenge	**and**	lose

Connection:

survival	**and**	direction

Connection:

conclude	**and**	direction

Connection:

Show You Know

Answer the questions below to show you know how each boldface Word Bank word is used.

1. Would climbing a mountain be a **challenge** for you? Explain why.

   _____

   _____

2. If you were stranded on a desert island, what would you need for

   survival? _____

   _____

3. You see pizza on the floor and on your dog's mouth. What might

   you **conclude?** Why? _____

   _____

Partner Up

If you are having trouble answering the questions, work with a partner. Use clues from the article to figure out word meanings you do not know.

Word Sort

Sort words from the article. Use the boxes below to sort nouns, verbs, and adjectives. Start with words from the Word Bank. Then look through the article to find other words to add.

Nouns	Verbs	Adjectives
direction	lose	

Now that you have sorted your words, pick two from different categories and use them both in one sentence. For a challenge, pick more than two words.

1. _____

   _____

2. _____

   _____

ALL IN THE FAMILY

Add *-ion* to the word *conclude* to turn the verb into a noun. Then try the reverse with *direction*.

conclude

conclusion

direction

_____

Write About It!

You have read an article about trust-building workshops. Now you will write about it. Read the writing prompt. It gives your writing assignment.

Writing Prompt

After reading "Building Trust and Replacing Fear," suppose that you attended a trust-building workshop. Write a letter to the camp director, telling whether you think the experience was successful. Use ideas from the article and at least one word from the Word Bank.

argue • game • issue • resist • search

WRITING RUBRIC

In your response, you should:

• Write a letter to a trust building camp director expressing your opinion on the camp's effectiveness.

• Use details from the article to support your opinion.

• Use at least one word from the Word Bank.

• Use correct grammar, usage, and mechanics.

Prewrite It

Once you are sure you understand the prompt, plan what you want to say.

1. Review your notes from the class discussion. Begin to list your ideas in the organizer.

2. Reread the article. Look for additional details to add to the organizer.

3. Look back at the organizer. Think about which ideas most support your opinion about trust-building workshops. These are the ideas you will want to include in your writing. Cross out the rest.

My Opinion of Trust-Building Workshops

_____

_____

_____

Here, write your opinion, or what you think about trust-building workshops.

Facts from the Article

_____

_____

_____

_____

_____

_____

Write facts from the article. Pick facts that support your opinion.

Draft It

Now use your plan to draft, or write, your letter. The writing frame below will help you.

1. Start by giving your opinion. You have three choices of opinion. Underline your choice.

2. Then give your reasons. Read the second sentence. Finish the letter by giving reasons for your opinion. Make sure you explain your opinion with ideas from the article.

Dear Camp Director,

I think that the trust-building camp I attended was

(very successful, somewhat successful, not successful).

I think this because _____

_____

_____

_____

_____

_____

_____

_____

If you have trouble putting your ideas into words, work with a partner. Tell your partner what you want to say. Ask the person to write it for you. Use the person's notes to help you write.

✔ **CHECKLIST**

Evaluate your writing. A score of "5" is excellent. A score of "1" means you need to do more work. Then ask a partner to rate your work.

1. **Does the letter give a clear opinion?**

   Me: 1 2 3 4 5
   Partner: 1 2 3 4 5

2. **Are there ideas from the article to explain the opinion?**

   Me: 1 2 3 4 5
   Partner: 1 2 3 4 5

3. **Is there at least one Word Bank word used?**

   Me: 1 2 3 4 5
   Partner: 1 2 3 4 5

4. **Are grammar, usage, and mechanics correct?**

   Me: 1 2 3 4 5
   Partner: 1 2 3 4 5

Check It and Fix It

After you have written your letter, check your work. Try to read it with a "fresh eye," imagining that you have never read it before.

1. Is everything written clearly and correctly? Use the checklist on the right to see.

2. Trade your work with a classmate. Talk over ways you both might improve your letters. Use the ideas to revise your work.

3. For help with grammar, usage, and mechanics, go to the Handbook on pages 189–226.

Building Trust and Replacing Fear   **49**

Vocabulary Workshop

Add these words to your personal word bank by practicing them.

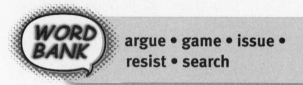

WORD BANK argue • game • issue • resist • search

Define It

Complete the chart below. First, tell what each Word Bank word means. Then, tell what the word does not mean. Use the example as a guide.

Your Choice

What other new words in the article would you like to remember? List them.

_____

_____

_____

Word	What It Is	What It Is Not
argue	to disagree about something	to cooperate or get along

Show You Know

Write a comic strip in the space below. Use all the Word Bank words in a way that shows you understand their meanings.

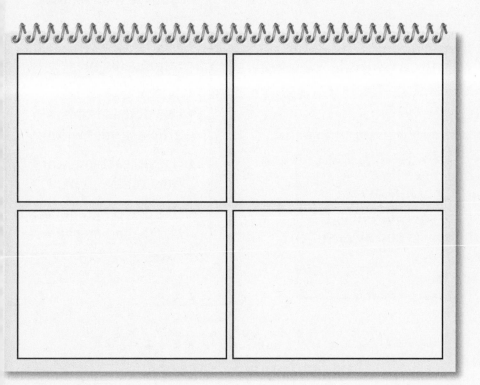

Word Sort

Use the chart to sort the words into nouns, verbs, and adjectives. Begin with the Word Bank words. Then choose other words to add to the chart.

Nouns	Verbs	Adjectives
	argue	

Now that you have sorted your words, pick two from different categories and use them both in one sentence. For a challenge, pick more than two words.

1. _____

_____

2. _____

Partner Up

Trade comic strips with a partner. Check each other's sentences. If something needs fixing, talk over how to fix it. Then make corrections.

ALL IN THE FAMILY

Adding -*ment* to a verb changes the word into a noun. Find a noun ending in -*ment* in the article. Write the verb and the noun formed by adding -*ment*.

argue

arguments

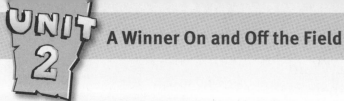

A Winner On and Off the Field

Write About It!

You have read an article about the challenges Alex Rodriguez faced. Now you will write about it. Read the writing prompt. It gives your writing assignment.

Writing Prompt

What do you think about the challenges that Alex Rodriguez faced? Imagine that Rodriguez is coming to your school to speak. Write a speech of introduction. Use ideas from the article and at least one word from the Word Bank.

battle • class • game • resolve • win

Prewrite It

Once you are sure you understand the prompt, plan what you want to say.

1. Review your notes from the class discussion. Jot down your thoughts on the sequence organizer.

2. Reread the article. Look for additional details about Alex Rodriguez and his life. Add to your organizer.

3. Your speech should give important facts about Rodriguez's life. You should also explain how conflicts in his life affected his character. Use the sequence organizer to decide which events in his life were most important. Circle them and cross out the rest.

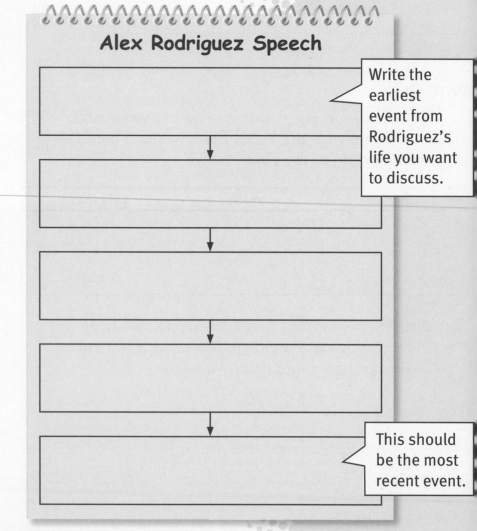

In your response, you should:

- Write a speech introducing Alex Rodriguez.
- Use details from the article in your writing.
- Use at least one word from the Word Bank.
- Use correct grammar, usage, and mechanics.

Alex Rodriguez Speech

Write the earliest event from Rodriguez's life you want to discuss.

This should be the most recent event.

Draft It

Now use your plan to draft, or write, your introduction. The writing frame below will help you.

1. Start with a detail that will capture your audience's attention and make them want to hear more about Rodriguez.

2. Remember to keep your tone respectful and professional. Follow the form to get started. Then include more details about Alex Rodriguez.

I would like to introduce Alex Rodriguez. One important thing

to know about Mr. Rodriguez is _____

_____

_____.

You should also know _____

_____

_____

_____

_____

_____

_____

Check It and Fix It

After you have written your introduction, check your work. You might read it out loud to see if it sounds like natural speech but also gives important facts about Rodriguez.

1. Is everything written clearly and correctly? Use the checklist on the right to see.

2. Trade drafts with a classmate. Talk over ways you both might improve your introductions. Use the ideas to revise your work.

3. For help with grammar, usage, and mechanics, go to the Handbook on pages 189–226.

If you are having trouble writing the introduction, think about using sequential order. Number the details you will use in the order that they happened. Use words like *first, next,* and *then* in your speech.

✔ CHECKLIST

Evaluate your writing. A score of "5" is excellent. A score of "1" means you need to do more work. Then ask a partner to rate your work.

1. **Does the introduction follow a logical order?**

   Me: 1 2 3 4 5
   Partner: 1 2 3 4 5

2. **Does the writing include information about Alex Rodriguez from the article?**

   Me: 1 2 3 4 5
   Partner: 1 2 3 4 5

3. **Is there at least one Word Bank word used?**

   Me: 1 2 3 4 5
   Partner: 1 2 3 4 5

4. **Are grammar, usage, and mechanics correct?**

   Me: 1 2 3 4 5
   Partner: 1 2 3 4 5

Vocabulary Workshop

Add these words to your personal word bank by practicing them.

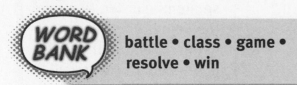 **WORD BANK** battle • class • game • resolve • win

Your Choice

What other new words in the article would you like to remember? List them.

_____

_____

_____

Define It

Complete the chart below. First, write what the Word Bank word means. Then write about a connection you have with the word. Use the example as a guide.

Word	What It Is	My Connection
battle	a fight or conflict	I like to battle with my friend in a game of chess.

Show You Know

Write a dialogue that uses three of the Word Bank words.
Show that you know what the Word Bank words mean.

_____ : _____
                   _____
_____ : _____
                   _____
_____ : _____
                   _____
_____ : _____
                   _____

Partner Up

Trade dialogues with a partner. Check each other's sentences. If something needs fixing, talk over how to fix it. Then make the corrections.

Word Play

If you want your writing to be lively and interesting, it helps to use words that are specific. Choose three of the Word Bank words, then list other words that mean about the same thing. Think about situations in which you would use each of these words.

Word Bank Words	Similar Words
battle	fight, conflict

Now choose two of your "new" words. Use each of them in a sentence.

1. _____

_____

2. _____

_____

Write About It!

You have read an article about pop icons in cultures around the world. Now you will write about them. Read the writing prompt. It gives your writing assignment.

Writing Prompt

After reading "World Pop Cultures," what do you think a pop icon can tell people about a culture? Choose a pop icon from a culture other than your own. Write a poem about it. Use ideas from the article and at least one word from the Word Bank.

clue • compete • conclude • convince • survival

WRITING RUBRIC

In your response, you should:

- Write a poem that describes a pop culture icon.

- Use details from the article in your poem.

- Use at least one word from the Word Bank.

- Use correct grammar, usage, and mechanics.

Prewrite It

Once you are sure you understand the prompt, plan what you want to say.

1. Review your notes from the class discussion. Write the name of the icon in the center of the web. On the web, jot down details about the cultural icon and what it tells you about the culture.

2. Reread the article. Look for additional details about the person and add them to the web.

3. You are writing a poem. Poems have descriptive words and phrases. Think about what ideas in your web will make the best description. Circle those ideas.

Draft It

Now use your web to draft, or write, your poem. The writing frame below will help you.

1. The title of your poem can be the name of your icon. Follow the "form" to create your poem. The last part, "Helps me understand," should tell details of what you know about the culture because of the icon.

2. Poems describe people or things by creating vivid images. Use words that make a clear picture for your readers.

_____

Looks like: _____

_____

Sounds like: _____

_____

Makes me feel: _____

_____

Helps me understand: _____

_____

_____

_____

Check It and Fix It

After you have written your poem, check your work. Look for vivid images that will make a clear picture in your readers' minds.

1. Is everything written clearly and correctly? Use the checklist on the right to see.

2. Trade your work with a classmate. Talk over ways you both might improve your poems. Use the ideas to revise your work.

3. For help with grammar, usage, and mechanics, go to the Handbook on pages 189–226.

Writing COACH

If you are unsure of what images to include, think about your five senses. What do you see when you see this icon? What do you hear? Smell? Feel?

✔ CHECKLIST

Evaluate your writing. A score of "5" is excellent. A score of "1" means you need to do more work. Then ask a partner to rate your work.

1. **Does the poem describe a pop icon?**

   Me: 1 2 3 4 5
   Partner: 1 2 3 4 5

2. **Does the poem explain what the icon helps people know about a culture?**

   Me: 1 2 3 4 5
   Partner: 1 2 3 4 5

3. **Is there at least one Word Bank word used?**

   Me: 1 2 3 4 5
   Partner: 1 2 3 4 5

4. **Are grammar, usage, and mechanics correct?**

   Me: 1 2 3 4 5
   Partner: 1 2 3 4 5

Vocabulary Workshop

Add these words to your personal word bank by practicing them.

 **clue • compete • conclude • convince • survival**

Define It

In the chart below, write a synonym for each Word Bank word. Then write an antonym. Remember, synonyms mean the same, or almost the same, thing. Antonyms have opposite meanings. Use the example to guide your work.

Word	Synonym	Antonym
clue	hint	answer

Your Choice

What other new words in the article would you like to remember? List them.

_____

_____

_____

If you have trouble thinking of synonyms and antonyms, try using a thesaurus. A thesaurus is a tool that lists synonyms and antonyms for words.

Show You Know

Write a short, short story (just a paragraph!) using the Word Bank words in the space below. Be sure your sentences show that you understand the meanings of the words.

Once upon a time _____

_____

_____

_____

_____

_____

_____

_____

_____

_____

Partner Up

Ask your partner to read your story. Your partner can answer these questions: *Does the story make sense? Does the story show that I know the meanings of the words?*

Word Endings: *-al*

- When you add the word ending *-al* to a verb, you change the verb (an action) into a noun (a thing).

  Verb: It is difficult for a plant to **survive** without water.
  Noun: Water the plants to help their **survival.**
  Verb: My sister will **deny** she broke Mom's vase.
  Noun: My mom probably will not believe her **denial.**

- Circle the correct form of the word in parentheses.

  What helps a pop icon to (survive, survival)? You cannot (deny, denial) that some icons seem to (survive, survival) for a long time. Their (survive, survival) probably depends on how popular and wealthy they are. I would (deny, denial) it, but I buy items featuring pop icons all the time.

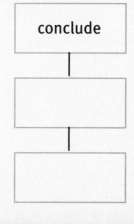

ALL IN THE FAMILY

Create two variations of the article word *conclude*. Add *-ing* to the end. Add the suffix *-ion* to the end.

conclude

Write About It!

You have read an article about ordinary kids who have become heroes. Now you will write about it. Read the writing prompt. It gives your writing assignment.

Writing Prompt

After reading "What Makes a Hero?" suppose that you are helping to create a Web page about kid heroes. Write a blog entry that would appear on the Web page. Use ideas from the article and at least one word from the Word Bank.

defend • discover • issue • negotiate • resist

WRITING RUBRIC

In your response, you should:

- Write a blog entry that expresses your feelings about the choices kid heroes make.

- Use details from the article.

- Use at least one word from the Word Bank.

- Use correct grammar, usage, and mechanics.

Prewrite It

Once you are sure you understand the prompt, plan what you want to say.

1. Review your notes from the class discussion. Begin to fill in the organizer with your feelings about kid heroes and the details that helped you come to this conclusion.

2. Reread the article. Look for additional details that you can add to the organizer.

3. Your blog entry expresses your opinion, but it should include details from the article that helped you form your ideas. Look at your organizer. Circle the details that are the most convincing or interesting.

Kid Heroes

My feelings or opinions about kid heroes:

Details from the article that helped me form my opinion:

Draft It

Now use your plan to draft, or write, your blog entry. The writing frame below will help you.

1. This blog gives your feelings or opinion. Start by stating how you feel about kid heroes.

2. Include details from the article that helped you form your feelings.

If you are having a hard time deciding what reasons to include in your blog entry, use a sentence frame: I think _____ because _____.

I feel that kid heroes are _____

_____

The reasons I feel this way are _____

_____

_____

_____

_____

_____

_____

_____

✔ **CHECKLIST**

Evaluate your writing. A score of "5" is excellent. A score of "1" means you need to do more work. Then ask a partner to rate your work.

1. **Does the blog entry share a feeling or opinion about kid heroes?**

   Me: 1 2 3 4 5
   Partner: 1 2 3 4 5

2. **Does the writing include information from the article that supports opinions or feelings?**

   Me: 1 2 3 4 5
   Partner: 1 2 3 4 5

3. **Is there at least one Word Bank term used?**

   Me: 1 2 3 4 5
   Partner: 1 2 3 4 5

4. **Are grammar, usage, and mechanics correct?**

   Me: 1 2 3 4 5
   Partner: 1 2 3 4 5

Check It and Fix It

After you have written your blog entry, check your work. Think about how it would "sound" if you found the information on a Web site. Does your writing seem like a blog entry?

1. Is everything written clearly and correctly? Use the checklist on the right to see.

2. Trade your work with a classmate. Talk over ways you both might improve your blog entries. Use the ideas to revise your work.

3. For help with grammar, usage, and mechanics, go to the Handbook on pages 189–226.

Vocabulary Workshop

Add these words to your personal word bank by practicing them.

WORD BANK defend • discover • issue • negotiate • resist

Define It

Write a Word Bank word on the line in each circle. You will need to use one word twice. Where the circles overlap, write something that shows how the paired words are the same or are related to each other. Write differences in the outer part of the circles.

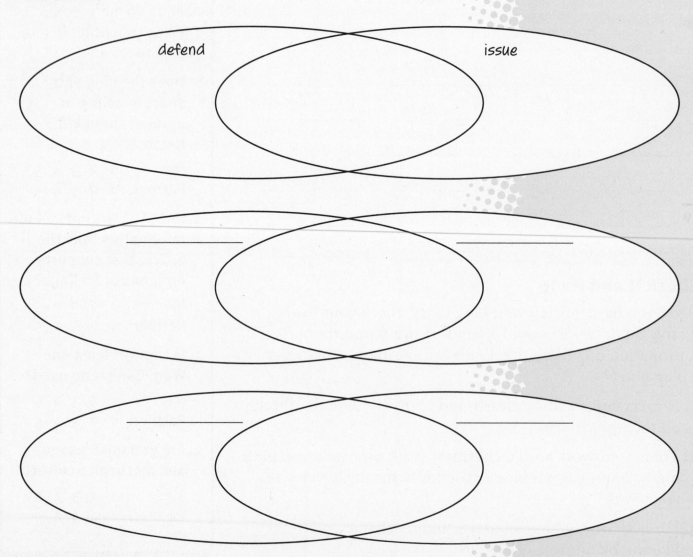

defend

issue

Show You Know

For three words from the Word Bank, write a clue sentence for a partner to see if he or she can match it with the correct term. See the example below for the word *discover*.

- If you find something that you never found before, you do this.

1. _____

   _____

2. _____

   _____

3. _____

   _____

Partner Up

Work with a partner to be sure that your clues make sense. If your partner cannot guess the correct word, ask for suggestions for rewriting your clue.

Word Play

Think about the words that you use in your writing. If you want your writing to be lively and interesting, it helps to use words that are specific. Choose three of the Word Bank words. List other words that mean about the same thing. Think about situations in which you would use these words.

Word Bank Words	Similar Words
negotiate	talk, discuss, bargain

Now choose two of your "new" words. Use each of them in a sentence.

1. _____

   _____

2. _____

   _____

UNIT 2
Krumping Contests

Write About It!

You have read an article about krumping contests. Now you will write about it. Read the writing prompt. It gives your writing assignment.

WRITING RUBRIC

In your response, you should:

- Tell why (or why not) people should support the krumping contest.

- Use details from the article to support your opinion.

- Use at least one word from the Word Bank.

- Use correct grammar, usage, and mechanics.

Writing Prompt

After reading "Krumping Contests," suppose you work for a local newspaper. A krumping contest will be held in your town. Write a press release to let people know why they should or should not support the contest. Use ideas from the article and at least one word from the Word Bank.

battle • challenge • convince • perform • win

Prewrite It

Once you are sure you understand the prompt, plan what you want to say.

1. Review your notes from the class discussion. Begin to list your ideas for the press release in the organizer.

2. Reread the article. Look for additional details to add to the organizer.

3. Look back at the organizer to decide if you are going to be for or against the krumping contest. Choose one "side" on your organizer. Think about which ideas most support your opinion. Cross out the rest.

Krumping Contest

Pros	Cons

Draft It

Now use your plan to draft, or write, your press release. The writing frame below will help you.

1. Start by giving your opinion. You have three choices of opinion. Underline your choice.

2. To finish the press release, give reasons for your opinion. Be sure to explain your opinion with ideas from the article.

To release to our readers: A krumping contest will soon be held in our town. You should (definitely support this, go to the contest if you have spare time, skip this contest completely). Here is why: _____

_____

_____

_____

_____

_____

_____

Check It and Fix It

After you have written your press release, check your work. Imagine that krumping contests are new to you and you are curious about why they do or do not deserve support.

1. Is everything written clearly and correctly? Use the checklist on the right to see.

2. Trade drafts with a classmate. Talk over ways you both might improve your press releases. Use the ideas to revise your work.

3. For help with grammar, usage, and mechanics, go to the Handbook on pages 189–226.

If you have trouble putting your ideas into words, work with a partner. Read your writing aloud and ask your partner for feedback. Continue reading aloud to see if the work sounds right.

✔ **CHECKLIST**

Evaluate your writing. A score of "5" is excellent. A score of "1" means you need to do more work. Then ask a partner to rate your work.

1. **Does the press release give an opinion?**

   Me: 1 2 3 4 5
   Partner: 1 2 3 4 5

2. **Does the press release include ideas from the article?**

   Me: 1 2 3 4 5
   Partner: 1 2 3 4 5

3. **Is there at least one Word Bank term used?**

   Me: 1 2 3 4 5
   Partner: 1 2 3 4 5

4. **Are grammar, usage, and mechanics correct?**

   Me: 1 2 3 4 5
   Partner: 1 2 3 4 5

Vocabulary Workshop

Add these words to your personal word bank by practicing them.

 battle • challenge • convince • perform • win

Define It

For each graphic organizer, choose two Word Bank words and put each word in a box. Then, in the third box, tell how those two words are connected. You will need to use one word twice. For example, *perform* and *win* are connected. If you *perform* well, you will *win*.

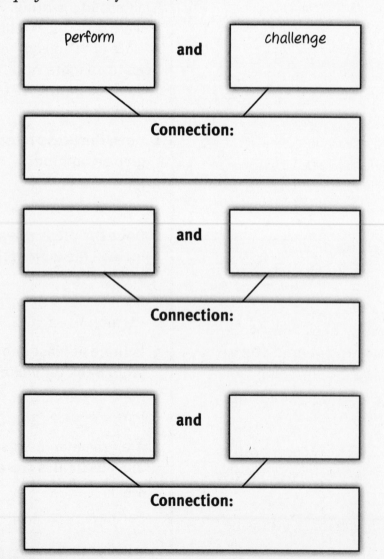

perform and challenge

Connection:

and

Connection:

and

Connection:

Your Choice

What other new words in the article would you like to remember? List them.

_____

_____

_____

Battle, *challenge*, and *win* can all name an action or a thing. Think about how the words can be used as you decide how they are connected.

Show You Know

Answer the questions below to show that you know the meaning of each boldface Word Bank word.

1. Who would be more likely to **battle**—teammates or opponents? Why?

   _____

   _____

2. What is something that would be a **challenge** for you? Why?

   _____

   _____

3. What is one situation in which you had to **convince** your parents of

   something? _____

   _____

4. In what type of activity are you able to **perform**? _____

   _____

Partner Up

Work with a partner to answer the questions. If you do not know what a word means, look at the Word Bank again and restate the meaning in your own words.

Word Endings: *-ance, -er*

- Adding *-ance* to a verb changes the verb (an action) into a noun (a thing).

  Verb: The dancers **perform** on Saturday.

  Noun: We are excited about their **performance**!

- Adding the ending *-er* to a word can change the meaning of the word to "a person who."

  Word without suffix: I hope all this practice helps me **win** the dance contest.

  Word with suffix: It would be great to be a **winner**!

- Circle the correct form of the word in parentheses.

  A famous (dance, dancer) is teaching a class at school. I would love to (perform, performance) with the dance group, so I am going to sign up for lessons. After six classes, we will give a (perform, performance, performer).

UNIT 2 WRAP UP

Writing Reflection

 Is conflict always bad?

Look through your writing from this unit and choose the best piece. Reflect on this piece of writing by completing each sentence below.

My best piece of writing from this unit is _____

_____

I chose this piece because _____

_____

_____

While I was writing, one goal I had was _____

_____

I accomplished this goal by _____

_____

_____

This writing helped me think more about the Big Question because

_____

_____

One thing I learned while writing that can help me in the future is

_____

_____

UNIT 3

What is important to know?

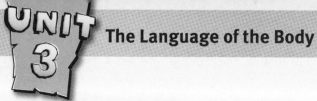

Write About It!

You have read an article about body language. Now you will write about it. Read the writing prompt. It gives your writing assignment.

Writing Prompt

After reading "The Language of the Body," what do you think about body language? Write an advice column for your school newspaper about how to read and interpret body language. Use ideas from the article and at least one word from the Word Bank.

distinguish • examine • imitate • observe • purpose

In your response, you should:

- Write an advice column about reading and interpreting body language.

- Give reasons for your advice based on the article you read.

- Use at least one word from the Word Bank.

- Use correct grammar, usage, and mechanics.

Prewrite It

Once you are sure you understand the prompt, plan what you want to say.

1. Review your notes from the class discussion. What advice would you give fellow students about reading body language? Take notes in the organizer.

2. Reread the article. Look for additional reasons that support your opinion. Add those to your organizer.

3. Take another look at your opinion. Do you need to change it after rereading? If so, make the changes. Read through the reasons you have listed. Which are strongest? Cross out reasons that are not as strong.

Advice Column

My Opinion

Your advice is what you think people should understand about body language.

Interpretations

Your interpretations are specific body language stances and what they might mean.

Draft It

Now use your plan to draft, or write, an advice column. The writing frame below will help you.

1. Start by writing down your advice. You have three choices of advice. Underline your choice.

2. Then give your support and examples. Start by finishing the second sentence below. Make sure you explain your reasons with ideas and examples from the article.

If you have trouble putting your ideas into words, work with a partner. Explain to your partner your idea. Have your partner repeat your idea back to you in his or her own words. Then write down the idea based on what you both said.

THIS JUST IN

How to Read and Interpret Body Language

A person's body language tells us (a lot, a little, nothing) about what that person is thinking or feeling. By learning to read and interpret body language, you can _____

_____

_____

_____

_____

_____

_____

_____

✔ CHECKLIST

Evaluate your writing. A score of "5" is excellent. A score of "1" means you need to do more work. Then ask a partner to rate your work.

1. **Does the column present advice clearly?**

   Me: 1 2 3 4 5
   Partner: 1 2 3 4 5

2. **Are there ideas from the article that support the advice?**

   Me: 1 2 3 4 5
   Partner: 1 2 3 4 5

3. **Is there at least one Word Bank word used?**

   Me: 1 2 3 4 5
   Partner: 1 2 3 4 5

4. **Are grammar, usage, and mechanics correct?**

   Me: 1 2 3 4 5
   Partner: 1 2 3 4 5

Check It and Fix It

After you have written your advice column, check your work. Imagine that you do not know anything about body language. Read to see if your writing gives useful information.

1. Is everything written clearly and correctly? Use the checklist on the right to see.

2. Exchange work with a classmate. Talk over ways to improve your advice columns. Use the ideas to revise your work.

3. For help with grammar, usage, and mechanics, go to the Handbook on pages 189–226.

Vocabulary Workshop

Add these words to your personal word bank by practicing them.

 **WORD BANK** **distinguish • examine • imitate • observe • purpose**

Define It

Choose two words from the Word Bank and write them on either side of the triangle below. Then describe how the two words are connected by completing the "because" portion of the sentence. Do this for three sets of words. You will have to use one word twice.

distinguish   **is connected to**   examine

because _in order to distinguish what something is you must examine it first._ _____

_____

is connected to

because _____

_____

is connected to

because _____

_____

Show You Know

Write a comic strip in the space below using all of the Word Bank words in a way that shows you understand the words.

Word Play

Using exact words in your writing can make what you have to say more lively, interesting, and detailed. In the chart below, list some additional specific words that mean the same or about the same as the Word Bank words. Think of words that give a precise meaning. Examples are shown.

Word Bank Words	Similar Words
imitate	copy, mimic
observe	
purpose	

Now try some of the new words. Rewrite each of the sentences, substituting one of your words for the boldface word.

1. I do not want to **imitate** what has already been invented.

_____

_____

2. Observe the way she reacts when I tell her the news.

_____

_____

3. Our team goal should have a clear **purpose**. _____

_____

Write About It!

You have read an article about having a part-time job while still in school. Now you will write about it. Read the writing prompt. It gives your writing assignment.

Writing Prompt

Imagine your high school is considering starting a work-study program. They have started an online blog for student feedback. Write a blog entry expressing your opinion on the issue. Use ideas from the article and at least one word from the Word Bank.

guess • judge • organize • probably • study

Prewrite It

Once you are sure you understand the prompt, plan what you want to say.

1. Review your notes from the class discussion. What do you think of the proposed work-study program? Jot down your notes on the organizer.

2. Reread the article. Look for additional reasons that support your opinion. Add those to your organizer.

3. Take another look at your opinion. Do you need to change it after rereading the article? If so, make the changes. Read through the reasons you have listed. Which are the strongest? Cross out the reasons that are not as strong.

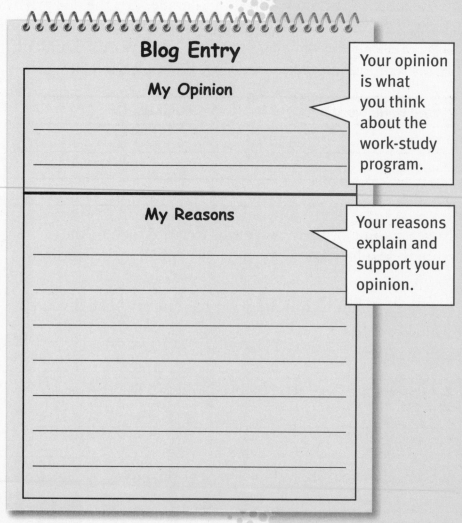

WRITING RUBRIC

In your response, you should:

- Write a blog entry expressing your opinion of your school's proposed work-study program.

- Give reasons for your opinion based on the article you read.

- Use at least one word from the Word Bank.

- Use correct grammar, usage, and mechanics.

Blog Entry

My Opinion

Your opinion is what you think about the work-study program.

My Reasons

Your reasons explain and support your opinion.

Draft It

Now use your plan to draft, or write, your blog entry. The writing frame below will help you.

1. Start by giving your opinion. You have three choices of opinion. Underline your opinion.

2. Then give reasons for your opinion. Make sure you explain your reasons with ideas from the article.

○ ○ ○

I think a work-study program for high school

students is a (good, interesting, horrible) idea.

I think this because _____

_____

_____

_____

_____

_____

_____

_____

_____

Check It and Fix It

After you have written your blog entry, check your work. Try to read it with a "fresh eye." Imagine that you have never read the letter before.

1. Is everything written clearly and correctly? Use the checklist on the right to see.

2. Trade your work with a classmate. Talk over ways you both might improve your blogs. Use the ideas to revise your work.

3. For help with grammar, usage, and mechanics, go to the Handbook on pages 189–226.

Writing COACH

If you have trouble putting your ideas into words, work with a partner. Read a sentence to your partner. See what your partner understood. Make corrections based on your partner's feedback.

✔ **CHECKLIST**

Evaluate your writing. A score of "5" is excellent. A score of "1" means you need to do more work. Then ask a partner to rate your work.

1. **Does the blog entry state an opinion clearly?**

   Me: 1 2 3 4 5
   Partner: 1 2 3 4 5

2. **Are there ideas from the article that explain the opinion?**

   Me: 1 2 3 4 5
   Partner: 1 2 3 4 5

3. **Is there at least one Word Bank word used?**

   Me: 1 2 3 4 5
   Partner: 1 2 3 4 5

4. **Are grammar, usage, and mechanics correct?**

   Me: 1 2 3 4 5
   Partner: 1 2 3 4 5

Vocabulary Workshop

Add these words to your personal word bank by practicing them.

WORD BANK guess • judge • organize • probably • study

Define It

Choose two words from the Word Bank and write them in the small boxes below. In the "Connection" box, describe how the two words are connected. Do this for three sets of words. You will have to use one word twice.

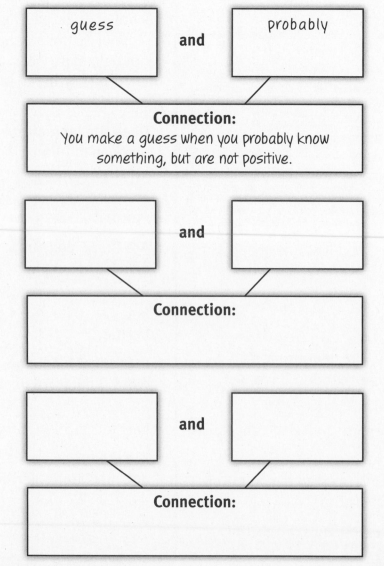

| guess | and | probably |

Connection:
You make a guess when you probably know something, but are not positive.

| | and | |

Connection:

| | and | |

Connection:

Your Choice

What other new words in the article would you like to remember? List them.

_____

_____

_____

Word COACH

The best way to remember new words is to use them soon after learning about them. Try to use one of your new words the next time you talk to someone. Use new words in and out of class.

Show You Know

Answer the questions below to show you know what each boldface Word Bank word means.

1. Why is a **guess** not a good way to make a decision? _____

   _____

2. What does it to mean to **judge** someone? _____

   _____

3. How can you tell if something is **organized**? _____

   _____

4. If something will **probably** happen, how likely is it to happen? _____

   _____

Word Endings: *-ment*

- When you add the word ending *-ment* to a verb, you change the word from an action to a thing, or noun.

  Verb: How would you **judge** the paintings?

  Noun: What is your **judgment** of the paintings?

- Circle the correct form of the words in parentheses.

  It is best not to (judge, judgment) people too quickly or harshly. If someone you know does something that, in your (judge, judgment), is not very wise, you may discover that there was a reason for it. Passing (judge, judgment) on people or situations without knowing all the facts can end up being embarrassing for you. The old saying is "do not (judge, judgment) unless you want to be (judge, judged, judgment)."

Knowing the root of a word can help you understand variations of the word. Come up with two variations of the word *guess*. Write them in the boxes below.

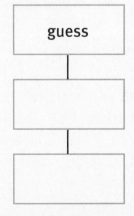

guess

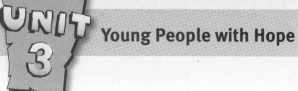

Write About It!

You have read an article about how young people today fight for racial justice. Now you will write about it. Read the writing prompt. It gives your writing assignment.

Writing Prompt

After reading "Young People with Hope," how are young people fighting racial injustice? Write a journal entry about how young people are—or can be—fighting for racial justice. Use ideas from the article and at least one word from the Word Bank.
demand • integrate • measure • narrow • purpose

In your response, you should:

• Write a personal journal entry about how young people are fighting for racial justice.

• Provide details based on the article you read.

• Use at least one word from the Word Bank.

• Use correct grammar, usage, and mechanics.

Prewrite It

Once you are sure you understand the prompt, plan what you want to say.

1. Review your notes from the class discussion. Have you heard about young people fighting for racial justice? Do you have any ideas about what could be done? Jot down your notes.

2. Reread the article. Look for additional ideas to include in your entry. Add to your organizer.

3. Look at your organizer. Do you see any patterns in what young people are doing? If so, put similar ideas together to organize them. Cross out ideas that are not as strong.

Fighting Racial Injustice

The Problem	What Young People Are Doing

Draft It

Now use your plan to draft, or write, a journal entry. The writing frame below will help you.

1. Start by stating what you've seen in your own life. You have three choices. Underline your choice.

2. Then give details, examples, and ideas about how young people can aid in fighting racial injustice. Read the second sentence below and finish the thought. Make sure you include ideas from the article in the journal entry.

Journal Entry

I have (never, occasionally, frequently) seen people my age

doing things to fight racial injustice. There are many things

we can do to help, such as _____

_____

_____

_____

_____

_____

_____

_____

Check It and Fix It

After you have written your journal entry, check your work. Look for ideas to fight racial injustice that will really work. Are the ideas organized in a way that makes sense?

1. Is everything written clearly and correctly? Use the checklist on the right to see.

2. Exchange work with a classmate. Talk over ways to improve your journal entries. Use the ideas to revise your work.

3. For help with grammar, usage, and mechanics, go to the Handbook on pages 189–226.

Writing COACH

Work with a partner if you are having trouble writing out your ideas. Read a sentence to your partner. See what your partner understood from your sentence. Make corrections based on your partner's feedback.

✔ **CHECKLIST**

Evaluate your writing. A score of "5" is excellent. A score of "1" means you need to do more work. Then ask a partner to rate your work.

1. **Does the journal entry present thoughts clearly?**

   Me: 1 2 3 4 5
   Partner: 1 2 3 4 5

2. **Are there ideas from the article that support the writer's ideas?**

   Me: 1 2 3 4 5
   Partner: 1 2 3 4 5

3. **Is there at least one Word Bank word used?**

   Me: 1 2 3 4 5
   Partner: 1 2 3 4 5

4. **Are grammar, usage, and mechanics correct?**

   Me: 1 2 3 4 5
   Partner: 1 2 3 4 5

Vocabulary Workshop

Add these words to your personal word bank by practicing them.

WORD BANK demand • integrate • measure • narrow • purpose

Your Choice

What other new words in the article would you like to remember? List them.

_____

_____

_____

Define It

Choose two words from the Word Bank and write them in the Venn diagram circles below. Where the circles intersect, describe how the two words could be connected. Do this for three sets of words. You will have to use one word twice.

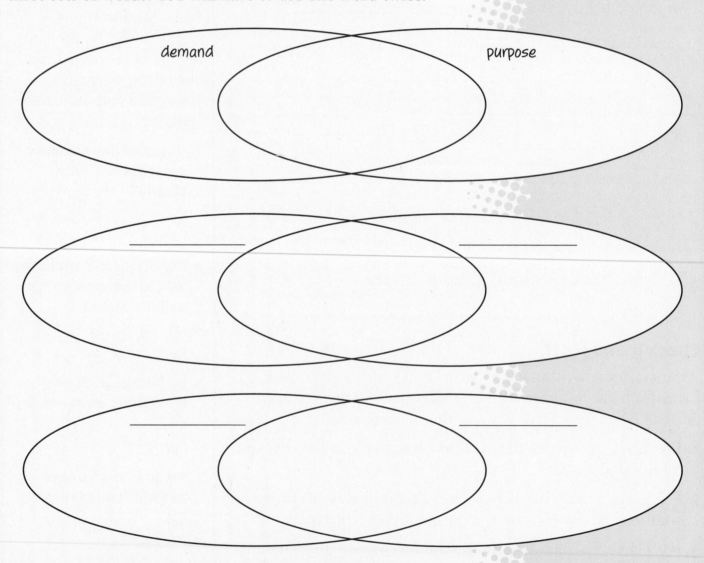

Show You Know

Write a short, short story (just one paragraph!) using the Word Bank words in the space below. Be sure your sentences show that you understand the meanings of the words. You can use Word Bank words more than once, but make sure you use them all at least once. Completing the sentence below should get you started.

We had decided as a group that we would _____

_____

_____

_____

Word Play

Using exact words in your writing can make what you say more lively, interesting, and detailed. In the chart below, list some additional words that mean the same or about the same as the Word Bank words. Examples are shown.

Word Bank Words	Similar Words
measure	check, figure
narrow	
purpose	

Now try out some of the words to see how they can make your writing more precise. Rewrite each of the sentences, substituting one of your words for the boldface word.

1. How will we **measure** our progress with this experiment?

_____

2. Our team had a **narrow** lead at half time. _____

_____

3. We have to have a clear and uniting **purpose**. _____

_____

Knowing the root of a word can help you understand variations of the word. Come up with two variations of the word *demand*. Write them in the boxes below.

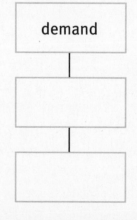

Write About It!

You have read an article about Major League baseball and commercialism. Now you will write about it. Read the writing prompt. It gives your writing assignment.

Writing Prompt

After reading "Major League Baseball and Money," do you think the sport has become too much about money or not? Write a dialogue where you and a friend debate the issue at a baseball game. Use ideas from the article and at least one word from the Word Bank.

establish • question • refer • source • support

In your response, you should:

• Write a dialogue debating two different opinions on baseball and commercialism.

• Give reasons for both opinions based on the article you read.

• Use at least one word from the Word Bank.

• Use correct grammar, usage, and mechanics.

Prewrite It

Once you are sure you understand the prompt, plan what you want to say.

1. Review your notes from the class discussion. To represent opposite views on baseball and money, jot down your notes on the organizer.

2. Reread the article. Look for additional reasons that support both views. Add those to your organizer.

3. Look at the opinions you jotted down. Do you need to change them after rereading the article? If so, make the changes. Read through the reasons you've listed. Which are strongest? Cross out the reasons that are not as strong.

Baseball Debate

My Opinion	Friend's Opinion

Opinions are what people think about a subject.

My Reasons	Friend's Reasons

Reasons explain or support the opinions.

Draft It

Now use your plan to draft, or write, a dialogue. The writing frame below will help you.

1. Start by stating both opinions in dialogue form. State your opinions for each speaker by underlining your choices.

2. Then give your reasons. Read the third sentence below. Finish the thought by giving a strong reason for your opinion. Then do the same for your friend's opinion. Make sure you explain the reasons with ideas from the article.

Me: I think Major League baseball (is, is not) way too much about money.

Friend: I do not agree. I think Major League baseball (is, is not) too much about money.

Me: I think this because _____

_____

_____

_____

_____

_____

_____

_____

Check It and Fix It

After you have written your dialogue, check your work. As you read, decide whether the dialogue is realistic. It should sound like real people speaking.

1. Is everything written clearly and correctly? Use the checklist on the right to see.

2. Trade your work with a classmate. Talk over ways to improve your dialogues. Use the ideas to revise your work.

3. For help with grammar, usage, and mechanics, go to the Handbook on pages 189–226.

Writing COACH

If you have trouble writing like someone would speak, work with a partner. Write down an idea and have your partner read it aloud. This can help make your writing sound like someone is speaking.

✔ CHECKLIST

Evaluate your writing. A score of "5" is excellent. A score of "1" means you need to do more work. Then ask a partner to rate your work.

1. **Does the dialogue state two opinions clearly?**

   Me: 1 2 3 4 5
   Partner: 1 2 3 4 5

2. **Are there ideas from the article that explain both opinions?**

   Me: 1 2 3 4 5
   Partner: 1 2 3 4 5

3. **Is there at least one Word Bank word used?**

   Me: 1 2 3 4 5
   Partner: 1 2 3 4 5

4. **Are grammar, usage, and mechanics correct?**

   Me: 1 2 3 4 5
   Partner: 1 2 3 4 5

Vocabulary Workshop

Add these words to your personal word bank by practicing them.

WORD BANK establish • question • refer • source • support

Your Choice

What other new words in the article would you like to remember? List them.

_____

_____

_____

Define It

Complete the chart below. First, tell what each Word Bank word means. Then write the context clues from the article that help you understand each word's meaning. Context clues are words or phrases around the word you do not know. Context words give you clues to the difficult word's meaning.

Word	Meaning	Context Clues
question	When you question something, you doubt its correctness.	Some fans question whether baseball is about the sport or making money.

Word COACH

When looking for context clues, certain key words can help you to understand the word you do not know. Words like *is, was, or, such as,* and *means* often point you to the meaning of the word you are having trouble with. For example: in the sentence, "One way to classify, or group, different kinds of cars is by engine," the word *or* points you to a definition of *classify*.

Show You Know

For three words from the Word Bank write a clue sentence for a partner to see if he or she can match it with the correct term. See the example below for the word *establish*.

- You do this if you create a new way to do something.

1. _____

   _____

2. _____

   _____

3. _____

   _____

Partner Up

Exchange your sentences with a partner and see how many you both get right. Afterward, look at the problem sentences and together come up with new clue sentences that would work better.

Word Sort

Sort the Word Bank words by category, using the boxes below. Some words can be nouns and verbs, depending on how you use them in a sentence. Read through the article and find additional words you can add to each box. Examples are shown.

Nouns	Verbs	Adjectives
question	question	

Now that you have sorted your words, pick two from different categories and combine them into a sentence. For a challenge, use more than two in a sentence.

1. _____

   _____

2. _____

   _____

UNIT 3 — City Life for Birds

Write About It!

You have read an article about whether birds in cities should be protected. Now you will write about it. Read the writing prompt. It gives your writing assignment.

Writing Prompt

Imagine you live in a big city. The local newspaper just ran a lengthy story about protecting urban birds. Write a letter to the editor expressing your support or disapproval. Use ideas from the article and at least one word from the Word Bank.

concept • devise • distinguish • guess • method

WRITING RUBRIC

In your response, you should:

- Write a letter to the editor expressing your support or disapproval for protecting urban birds.

- Give reasons for your decision based on the article you read.

- Use at least one word from the Word Bank.

- Use correct grammar, usage, and mechanics.

Prewrite It

Once you are sure you understand the prompt, plan what you want to say.

1. Review your notes from the class discussion. Do you think cities should do more to protect urban birds? Jot down your notes on the organizer.

2. Reread the article. Look for additional reasons that support your opinion. Add those to your organizer.

3. Look at your opinion. Do you need to change it after rereading the article? If so, make the changes. Read through the reasons you've listed. Which are the strongest? Cross out the reasons that are not as strong.

Letter to the Editor

My Opinion

> Your opinion is how you feel about the subject.

My Reasons

> Your reasons explain and support your opinion.

Draft It

Now use your plan to draft, or write, a letter to the editor. The writing frame below will help you.

1. Start by stating your opinion. You have three choices. Underline your choice.

2. Then give your reasons. Finish the thought by giving a strong reason for your opinion. Make sure you explain your reason with ideas from the article.

Dear Editor,

After reading your story on protecting urban birds, I think

the city (should do much more, is doing enough, should not

bother) to protect wild birds in the city. I feel this way because

_____

_____

_____

_____

_____

_____

_____

_____

Check It and Fix It

After you have written your letter to the editor, check your work. Imagine you are the editor receiving the letter. Are the arguments convincing enough?

1. Is everything written clearly and correctly? Use the checklist on the right to see.

2. Trade your work with a classmate. Talk over ways to improve your letters. Use the ideas to revise your work.

3. For help with grammar, usage, and mechanics, go to the Handbook on pages 189–226.

Writing COACH

If you have trouble putting your ideas into words, work with a partner. Read a sentence to your partner. See what your partner understood. This can help you to figure out where your writing needs to be clearer.

✔ CHECKLIST

Evaluate your writing. A score of "5" is excellent. A score of "1" means you need to do more work. Then ask a partner to rate your work.

1. Does the letter state an opinion clearly?

Me: 1 2 3 4 5
Partner: 1 2 3 4 5

2. Are there ideas from the article that help explain the opinion?

Me: 1 2 3 4 5
Partner: 1 2 3 4 5

3. Is there at least one Word Bank word used?

Me: 1 2 3 4 5
Partner: 1 2 3 4 5

4. Are grammar, usage, and mechanics correct?

Me: 1 2 3 4 5
Partner: 1 2 3 4 5

Vocabulary Workshop

Add these words to your personal word bank by
practicing them.

 **WORD BANK** concept • devise •
distinguish • guess • method

Your Choice

What other new words in
the article would you like
to remember? List them.

_____

_____

_____

Define It

Choose two words from the Word Bank and write them in
the small boxes below. In the "Connection" box, describe
how the two words are connected. Do this for three sets of
words. You will have to use one word twice.

devise	**and**	method

Connection:

	and	

Connection:

	and	

Connection:

Show You Know

Answer the questions below to show you know what each boldface Word Bank word means.

1. If you understand something's **concept**, it means you understand what? _____

_____

2. What does it mean if you **devise** a plan? _____

_____

3. What does it mean if you have a **method** for doing your

homework? _____

_____

Partner Up

Trade your answers with a partner. Check each other's answers to see if they make sense. Are there any problems in the writing that need to be fixed? If so, talk over how to fix them. Then make the corrections.

Word Sort

Sort the Word Bank words by category, using the boxes below. Some words can be nouns and verbs, depending on how you use them in a sentence. Read through the article and find additional words you can add to each box. Examples are shown.

Nouns	Verbs	Adjectives
guess	guess	

Now that you have sorted your words, pick two from different categories and combine them into a sentence. For a challenge, pick more than two to use in a sentence.

1. _____

_____

2. _____

_____

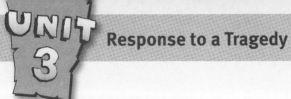

Write About It!

You have read an article about how a community responded to a tragedy. Now you will write about it. Read the writing prompt. It gives your writing assignment.

Writing Prompt

After reading "Response to a Tragedy," write a poem to a community that has experienced a tragedy, expressing what you learned from their reaction. Use ideas from the article and at least one word from the Word Bank.

form • knowledge • observe • question • report

Prewrite It

Once you are sure you understand the prompt, plan what you want to say.

1. Review your notes from the class discussion. Think about the way Huntington responded to the fatal plane crash. Jot down your thoughts in the organizer.

2. Reread the article. Look for additional ideas to describe in your poem. Add those to your organizer.

3. Look at your organizer. Are there ideas that seem to stand out? Are there strong expressions that you want to include? If so, underline the most effective language. Cross out ineffective language.

WRITING RUBRIC

In your response, you should:

- Write a poem to a community that has experienced a tragedy, expressing what you learned from their reaction.

- Use ideas from the article you read to explain your feelings.

- Use at least one word from the Word Bank.

- Use correct grammar, usage, and mechanics.

Reaction	Inspiration

What were people thinking and feeling after the tragedy occurred?

What inspired you about the way the people responded to tragedy?

Draft It

Now use your plan to draft, or write, a poem. The writing frame below will help you.

1. Start by recognizing what people in the community must have felt when they learned of the tragedy. Use the first line as a way to get started. Remember: Poems do not have to rhyme. Expressing true emotion is the goal.

2. Then describe how the community reacted. These are the things that inspired you. Use the second sentence below to help give you some direction. Keep in mind the notes you made from the article.

When I heard the tragic news, _____

_____

_____

_____

When I saw your whole community _____

_____

_____

_____

_____

_____

Check It and Fix It

After you have written your poem, check your work. Look for interesting words and images that bring the ideas in your poem "to life."

1. Is everything written clearly and correctly? Use the checklist on the right to see.

2. Exchange your work with a classmate and talk over ways you both might improve the descriptive language in your poems. Use the ideas to revise your work.

3. For help with grammar, usage, and mechanics, go to the Handbook on pages 189–226.

✔ CHECKLIST

Evaluate your writing. A score of "5" is excellent. A score of "1" means you need to do more work. Then ask a partner to rate your work.

1. **Does the poem clearly describe what was inspirational?**

   Me: 1 2 3 4 5
   Partner: 1 2 3 4 5

2. **Are there ideas from the article that help the description?**

   Me: 1 2 3 4 5
   Partner: 1 2 3 4 5

3. **Is there at least one Word Bank word used?**

   Me: 1 2 3 4 5
   Partner: 1 2 3 4 5

4. **Are grammar, usage, and mechanics correct?**

   Me: 1 2 3 4 5
   Partner: 1 2 3 4 5

Vocabulary Workshop

Add these words to your personal word bank by practicing them.

WORD BANK

form • knowledge • observe • question • report

Define It

Complete the chart below. First, tell what the Word Bank word means. Then, tell what the word does not mean. Use the example as a guide.

Word	What It Is	What It Is Not
form	to make something or organize something	a disorganized mess

Word COACH

An antonym is a word that means the opposite. For example, *hot* is an antonym for *cold*. It is sometimes helpful to describe something by what it is not. Try to describe someone you know using only antonyms.

Show You Know

To show that you understand the Word Bank words, write four sentences. In each sentence, use and highlight two of the words. You will use some words more than once, but be sure to use each Word Bank word at least once. Use the example as a model.

- Knowledge can be gained when you observe people or situations.

1. _____

   _____

2. _____

   _____

3. _____

   _____

4. _____

   _____

Partner Up

To check your work, first trade sentences with a different partner. Make changes based on your partner's feedback.

Word Endings: *-able*

- When you add the word ending *-able* to a word, you change the word into an adjective, or descriptive word.

  Noun: Your **knowledge** of history is impressive.
  Adjective: He is very **knowledgeable** about history.

- Circle the correct form of the words in parentheses.

  I think some of her facts are (questionable, question). I know she is very (knowledge, knowledgeable) about the subject. But some of her (observables, observations) do not even seem (reportable, report). Are UFOs really (observation, observable)?

ALL IN THE FAMILY

Knowing the root of a word can help you understand variations of the word. Come up with two variations of the word *know*. Write them in the boxes below.

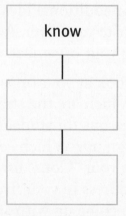

know

Write About It!

You have read an article about wilderness training programs for kids. Now you will write about it. Read the writing prompt. It gives your writing assignment.

WRITING RUBRIC

In your response, you should:

- Write a flyer to post at your school for a summer wilderness training camp.

- Use specific ideas from the article to create your summary.

- Use at least one word from the Word Bank.

- Use correct grammar, usage, and mechanics.

Writing Prompt

After reading "Wilderness Learning," you have been asked to write a flyer to post at your school for such a camp. No matter how you feel about these camps, you need to get the word out to your fellow students. Use ideas from the article and at least one word from the Word Bank.

arrange • judge • knowledge • limit • purpose

Prewrite It

Once you are sure you understand the prompt, plan what you want to say.

1. Review your notes from the class discussion. Think about what would appeal to students most about this camp. Jot your ideas in the organizer.

2. Reread the article. Look for additional ideas to write your flyer. Add those to your organizer.

3. Look at your organizer. Which are the strongest reasons for students to sign up? Which concerns in your "Cons" list can you address in your flyer? Try to come up with answers for the biggest concerns.

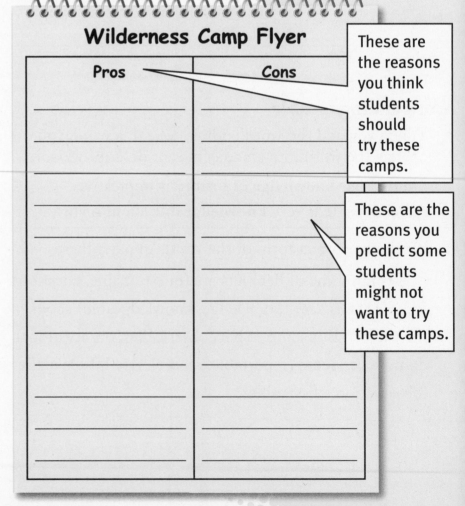

Wilderness Camp Flyer

Pros	Cons

These are the reasons you think students should try these camps.

These are the reasons you predict some students might not want to try these camps.

Draft It

Now use your plan to draft, or write, the flyer. The writing frame below will help you.

1. Start out with an interesting question to grab students' attention. You have three choices. Underline your choice.

2. Then provide detailed information about what goes on at a wilderness camp. Be sure to address some of the concerns you noted in your organizer and to use ideas from the article.

Do you know (how to build a shelter?, what plants are

safe to eat?, how to climb a mountain?) Why spend all

summer bored with nothing to do when you could

_____

_____

_____

_____

_____

_____

_____

_____

Check It and Fix It

After you have written your flyer, check your work. Imagine that you do not know anything about survival camps. Does the flyer give enough information for readers?

1. Is everything written clearly and correctly? Use the checklist on the right to see.

2. Exchange your work with a classmate and talk over ways you both might improve the information on your flyers. Use the ideas to revise your work.

3. For help with grammar, usage, and mechanics, go to the Handbook on pages 189–226.

If you have trouble putting your ideas into words, work with a partner. Explain to your partner your idea. Have your partner repeat your idea back to you in his or her own words. Then, write down the idea based on what you both said.

✔ CHECKLIST

Evaluate your writing. A score of "5" is excellent. A score of "1" means you need to do more work. Then ask a partner to rate your work.

1. Does the flyer present the information clearly?

Me: 1 2 3 4 5
Partner: 1 2 3 4 5

2. Are there ideas from the article that help the description?

Me: 1 2 3 4 5
Partner: 1 2 3 4 5

3. Is there at least one Word Bank word used?

Me: 1 2 3 4 5
Partner: 1 2 3 4 5

4. Are grammar, usage, and mechanics correct?

Me: 1 2 3 4 5
Partner: 1 2 3 4 5

Vocabulary Workshop

Add these words to your personal word bank by practicing them.

 **arrange • judge • knowledge • limit • purpose**

Define It

Choose two words from the Word Bank and write them on either side of the triangle below. Then describe how the two words are connected by completing the "because" portion of the sentence. Do this for three sets of words. You will have to use one word twice.

arrange — is connected to — purpose

_____ / \ _____

because _____

_____

is connected to

_____ / \ _____

because _____

_____

is connected to

_____ / \ _____

because _____

_____

Show You Know

Write a comic strip in the space below using all of the Word Bank words in a way that shows you understand the words.

Word Play

Using exact words in your writing can make what you say more lively, interesting, and detailed. In the chart below, list some additional specific words that mean the same or about the same as the Word Bank words. Think of words that give a precise meaning. An example is shown.

Word Bank Words	Similar Words
judge	figure out
limit	
purpose	

Rewrite each of the sentences below, substituting one of your words for the boldface word.

1. It is hard to **judge** how long the event will last. _____

_____

2. We need to **limit** the number of people who can sign up.

_____

_____

3. What is the **purpose** of this organization? _____

_____

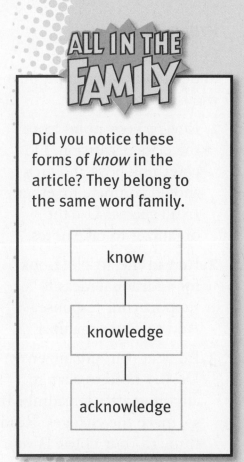

ALL IN THE FAMILY

Did you notice these forms of *know* in the article? They belong to the same word family.

know

knowledge

acknowledge

Write About It!

You have read an article about gender stereotypes in sports. Now you will write about it. Read the writing prompt. It gives your writing assignment.

WRITING RUBRIC

Writing Prompt

Imagine your community is thinking of combining boys and girls teams into one league. They want members of the community to write a one-paragraph response to this idea. Use ideas from the article and at least one word from the Word Bank.

concept • examine • involve • narrow • study

In your response, you should:

- Write a one-paragraph response to combining boys and girls sports teams.

- Use specific ideas from the article in your response.

- Use at least one word from the Word Bank.

- Use correct grammar, usage, and mechanics.

Prewrite It

Once you are sure you understand the prompt, plan what you want to say.

1. Review your notes from the class discussion. Do you think boys and girls should compete together? In all sports? Use the organizer to take notes.

2. Reread the article. Look for additional ideas to support your response. Add to your organizer.

3. Look at your organizer. Do you need to change anything after rereading? If so, make the changes. Read through your notes. Is your response clear? Do you have good support notes? Cross out the notes that are not as strong.

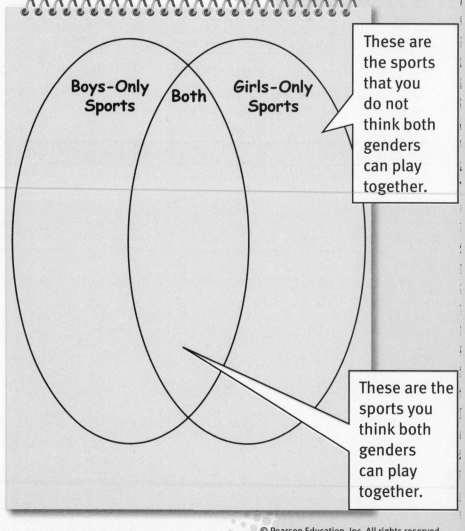

Boys-Only Sports   Both   Girls-Only Sports

These are the sports that you do not think both genders can play together.

These are the sports you think both genders can play together.

Draft It

Now use your plan to draft, or write, your response. The writing frame below will help you.

1. Start by stating what you think of combining boys and girls teams. You have three choices. Underline your choice.

2. Then give strong reasons for your opinion. Make sure you explain your reasons with ideas from the article.

I think combining girls and boys on the same teams is a

(terrible, possible, great) idea. I think this because _____

_____

_____

_____

_____

_____

_____

_____

_____

_____

_____

Work with a partner to make sure your response and the reasons for your response are clear. Read a sentence to your partner. See what your partner understood from your sentence. Make corrections based on your partner's feedback.

✔ CHECKLIST

Evaluate your writing. A score of "5" is excellent. A score of "1" means you need to do more work. Then ask a partner to rate your work.

1. **Do the reasons given help support the response?**

   Me: 1 2 3 4 5
   Partner: 1 2 3 4 5

2. **Are there ideas from the article in the response?**

   Me: 1 2 3 4 5
   Partner: 1 2 3 4 5

3. **Is there at least one Word Bank word used?**

   Me: 1 2 3 4 5
   Partner: 1 2 3 4 5

4. **Are grammar, usage, and mechanics correct?**

   Me: 1 2 3 4 5
   Partner: 1 2 3 4 5

Check It and Fix It

After you have written your response, check your work. Imagine that you do not have an opinion about the subject. Does your writing give strong reasons to help you form an opinion?

1. Is everything written clearly and correctly? Use the checklist on the right to see.

2. Exchange your work with a classmate and talk over ways to improve your responses. Use the ideas to revise your work.

3. For help with grammar, usage, and mechanics, go to the Handbook on pages 189–226.

Vocabulary Workshop

Add these words to your personal word bank by practicing them.

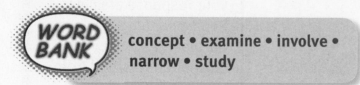

WORD BANK concept • examine • involve • narrow • study

Your Choice

What other new words in the article would you like to remember? List them.

_____

_____

_____

Define It

Complete the chart below. First, tell what the Word Bank word means. Then describe your connection to the word. It can be a memory, or it can be what the word makes you think of when you read or hear it. Use the example as a guide.

Word	What It Is	My Connection
concept	the idea you have about something based on information	I think of music albums that are based on one concept.

Show You Know

For three words from the Word Bank, write a clue sentence for a partner to see if he or she can match it with the correct term. See the example below for the word *examine*.

- If you are a detective, you do this to the evidence.

1. _____

   _____

2. _____

   _____

3. _____

   _____

Partner Up

After you write your clue sentences, trade them with a partner. Check each other's answers to make sure you both got them right. Then try to come up with a couple of extras using variations of the Word Bank words found in the article. For example, use *examination* or *preconceived* in a clue sentence.

Word Sort

Sort the Word Bank words by category, using the boxes below. Read through the article and find additional words you can add to each box. Look for variations of the Word Bank words. Examples are shown.

Nouns	Verbs	Adjectives
concept		narrow

Now that you have sorted your words, pick two from different categories and combine them into a sentence. For a challenge, use more than two in a sentence.

1. _____

   _____

2. _____

   _____

Writing Reflection

 What is important to know?

Look through your writing from this unit and choose the best piece. Reflect on this piece of writing by completing each sentence below.

My best piece of writing from this unit is _____

_____

I chose this piece because _____

_____

_____

While I was writing, one goal I had was _____

_____

I accomplished this goal by _____

_____

_____

This writing helped me think more about the Big Question because

_____

_____

One thing I learned while writing that can help me in the future is

_____

_____

 Do we need words to communicate well?

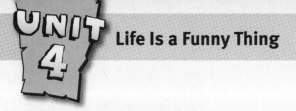

Write About It!

You have read an article about ways people show humor without using words. Now you will write about it. Read the writing prompt. It gives your writing assignment.

In your response, you should:

- Write a sketch based on nonverbal humor.

- Use details from the article.

- Use at least one word from the Word Bank.

- Use correct grammar, usage, and mechanics.

Writing Prompt

After reading "Life Is a Funny Thing," what do you think can make a situation funny, even if there are no words? Write a short comedy sketch that involves only nonverbal humor. Use ideas from the article and at least one word from the Word Bank.

expression • gesture • nonverbal • reveal

Prewrite It

Once you are sure you understand the prompt, plan what you want to say.

1. Review your notes on nonverbal comedy from the class discussion. Jot down your thoughts in the organizer.

2. Reread the article. Look for additional details about the different parts of physical comedy.

3. Think about your own comedy sketch. What parts of physical comedy are you going to use in your writing? Circle the ideas that you are sure you want to include.

Components of Physical Comedy

Gestures	Expressions	Body Language

Draft It

Now use your plan to draft, or write, your comedy sketch. The writing frame below will help you.

1. Your comedy sketch should show a funny situation that does not use words. Look at the Real-Life Connection on page 111 in your Anthology for an example.

2. Write your sketch. Then explain what message is sent.

If you are having trouble, work with a partner. Read the situation to see if it is humorous. If your partner does not understand, adjust your writing with your partner's help.

Comedy Sketch

_____

_____

_____

_____

Message It Sends

_____

_____

_____

_____

✔ CHECKLIST

Evaluate your writing. A score of "5" is excellent. A score of "1" means you need to do more work. Then ask a partner to rate your work.

1. **Does the sketch portray a humorous situation?**

   Me: 1 2 3 4 5
   Partner: 1 2 3 4 5

2. **Does the sketch use details from the article about physical comedy?**

   Me: 1 2 3 4 5
   Partner: 1 2 3 4 5

3. **Is there at least one Word Bank word used?**

   Me: 1 2 3 4 5
   Partner: 1 2 3 4 5

4. **Are grammar, usage, and mechanics correct?**

   Me: 1 2 3 4 5
   Partner: 1 2 3 4 5

Check It and Fix It

After you have written your comedy sketch, check your work. You could even act it out.

1. Is the sketch written clearly? Use the checklist on the right to see.

2. Trade your work with a classmate. See if your partner can understand why the situation you wrote about is humorous. Use the ideas to revise your work.

3. For help with grammar, usage, and mechanics, go to the Handbook on pages 189–226.

Vocabulary Workshop

Add these words to your personal word bank by practicing them.

expression • gesture • nonverbal • reveal

Your Choice

What other new words in the article would you like to remember? List them.

_____

_____

_____

Define It

Complete the chart below. First, give a real-life example of the Word Bank word. Then, tell your connection to the word. Use the example as a guide.

Word	Meaning	Connection
expression	a look or an action that shows feeling or thought	I had a joyful expression on my face when I got a new skateboard.

Show You Know

To show that you understand the Word Bank words, write two sentences. In each sentence, use and highlight two of the Word Bank words. Use the example as a model.

- A hug is a gesture that can reveal love.

1. _____

_____

2. _____

_____

Partner Up

Trade sentences with a partner. Check to see if the sentences make sense. If not, suggest ways to fix them.

Word Endings: *-ing, -ly*

- Adding *-ly* to an adjective can change the adjective to an adverb. Adjectives describe nouns. Adverbs describe verbs or adjectives.

Adjective: A smile is a **nonverbal** way to show you are happy.

Adverb: Her expression showed me **nonverbally** that she liked the gift.

- Adding *-ing* to a verb can sometimes turn the verb into an adjective.

Verb: Be careful not to **reveal** the surprise!

Adjective: Your giggles might be **revealing**.

- Circle the correct form of the word in parentheses.

How can you (nonverbal, nonverbally) show friendship to someone? One way to (reveal, revealing) your true feelings is to pat a friend on the back if she feels sad. A kind smile is also (reveal, revealing). Of course, if your (nonverbal, nonverbally) gestures do not get the message across, you can always say something kind!

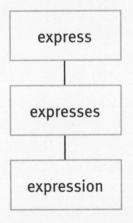

Did you notice these forms of *express* in the article? They belong to the same word family.

express
expresses
expression

Write About It!

You have read an article about urban street dancing. Now you will write about it. Read the writing prompt. It gives your writing assignment.

Writing Prompt

Imagine that you are writing for a stepping Web site. Write a blog entry explaining whether you think street dancing is meaningful. Use ideas from the article and at least one word from the Word Bank.
communication • language • nonverbal • symbolize

In your answer, you should:

• Tell whether street dancing is meaningful.

• Use details from the article in your writing.

• Use at least one word from the Word Bank.

• Use correct grammar, usage, and mechanics.

Prewrite It

Once you are sure you understand the prompt, plan what you want to say.

1. Review your notes from the class discussion. At the top of the organizer, circle the choice that gives your opinion about street dancing.

2. Reread the article. Look for additional details to support your opinion about street dancing, and add them to your organizer. Be sure to explain each reason.

3. Look for the reasons that will best support your opinion about street dancing. Circle those that you wish to use in your writing.

My opinion: Street dancing (is, is not) meaningful.

Reasons	Explanations

Draft It

Now use your plan to draft, or write, your blog entry.
The writing frame below will help you.

1. Start by circling one of the choices in the first sentence.

2. In the rest of the blog entry, include reasons that support
   your opinion. Draw ideas from the article to show why
   street dancing is or is not meaningful.

○ ○ ○ ○

I think street dancing (is, is not) meaningful. My

reasons include _____

_____

_____

_____

_____

_____

_____

_____

**Your writing supports
your opinion about street
dancing. Check back
through to be sure that
your reasons support your
opinion. If you find a reason
that does not support
your opinion well, make it
stronger or remove it.**

✔ *CHECKLIST*

Evaluate your writing.
A score of "5" is excellent.
A score of "1" means you
need to do more work.
Then ask a partner to rate
your work.

1. **Does the blog entry
   include an opinion
   about street dancing?**

   Me: 1 2 3 4 5
   Partner: 1 2 3 4 5

2. **Does the writing
   include information
   about street dancing
   from the article?**

   Me: 1 2 3 4 5
   Partner: 1 2 3 4 5

3. **Is there at least one
   Word Bank word used?**

   Me: 1 2 3 4 5
   Partner: 1 2 3 4 5

4. **Are grammar, usage,
   and mechanics correct?**

   Me: 1 2 3 4 5
   Partner: 1 2 3 4 5

Check It and Fix It

After you have written your blog entry, look over your work.
Imagine that your audience is not familiar with street dancing.
Be sure the reasons for your opinion make sense.

1. Is everything written clearly and correctly? Use the checklist
   on the right to see.

2. Trade blog entries with a classmate. Talk over ways to
   improve your entries. Use the ideas to revise your work.

3. For help with grammar, usage, and mechanics, go to the
   Handbook on pages 189–226.

Vocabulary Workshop

Add these words to your personal word bank by practicing them.

 **WORD BANK** communicate • language • nonverbal • symbolize

Your Choice

What other new words in the article would you like to remember? List them.

_____

_____

_____

Define It

Look at each pair of Word Bank words. Explain how the two words might be connected. For example, how might *communicate* and *nonverbal* be connected? A nod is one *nonverbal* way to *communicate*.

communicate	**and**	language

Connection:

symbolize	**and**	language

Connection:

nonverbal	**and**	symbolize

Connection:

Show You Know

For three words from the Word Bank, write a clue sentence for a partner to see if he or she can match it with the correct word. See the example for the word *nonverbal*.

- This describes a way to communicate without words.

1. _____
_____

2. _____
_____

3. _____
_____

Partner Up

Trade your answers with a partner. Check each other's clues to see if they make sense. If there are any problems, work with your partner to make corrections.

Word Endings: *-ize*

- When you add the ending *-ize* to a noun or an adjective, you create a verb.

  Noun: The dove is a **symbol** of peace.

  Verb: What other objects **symbolize** peace?

- In the chart below, add *-ize* to each noun to make a verb. An example is shown.

Noun	Verb
apology	apologize
formal	
real	
sympathy	

Choose one of the nouns and one of the verbs and use them each in a sentence.

1. _____
_____

2. _____
_____

Look through the article to find two other words in the same word family as *communicate*. Write them in the boxes.

communicate

_____

_____

Dancing in the Streets   **111**

Just Add Ads

Write About It!

You have read an article about advertising. Now you will write about it. Read the writing prompt. It gives your writing assignment.

Writing Prompt

After reading "Just Add Ads," what do you think makes an ad effective? Analyze an ad of your choice from a source like television, the Internet, or a magazine. The ad should include images. Use ideas from the article and at least one word from the Word Bank.

correspond • message • share • visual

In your response, you should:

- Write an analysis of an ad.
- Include ideas from the article about the ad's images.
- Use at least one word from the Word Bank.
- Use correct grammar, usage, and mechanics.

Prewrite It

Once you are sure you understand the prompt, plan what you want to say.

1. Review your notes from the class discussion. Then choose an advertisement to analyze. The ad should include images.

2. Reread the article. Look for details about advertising.

3. Think about what the article says about advertising as you examine your advertisement. Answer the questions in the organizer about your ad.

Analyze an Ad

What product is being advertised?
What words give information?
What words persuade readers?
What ideas are shown in images?

Draft It

Now use your plan to draft, or write, your analysis.
The writing frame below will help you.

1. Begin by telling what advertisement you are analyzing.
   Circle the choice that gives your opinion.

2. Explain how the words and images give a message about
   the product. Be sure to support your opinion about the ad.

I looked at an ad that is advertising _____

I think this ad (is, is not) effective because _____

_____

_____

_____

_____

_____

_____

_____

_____

_____

_____

Check It and Fix It

After you have written your analysis, check your work. Read it
with a "fresh eye," being sure that your analysis gives reasons
for your opinion.

1. Is everything written clearly and correctly? Use the checklist
   on the right to see.

2. Trade your work with a classmate. Talk over ways to
   improve your analyses. Use the ideas to revise your work.

3. For help with grammar, usage, and mechanics, go to the
   Handbook on pages 189–226.

Remember that you are
analyzing an ad, not
selling the product.
Be sure that readers will
understand whether or
not the ad is effective.

✔ CHECKLIST

Evaluate your writing.
A score of "5" is excellent.
A score of "1" means you
need to do more work.
Then ask a partner to rate
your work.

1. **Does the analysis
   name the product
   and tell whether the
   advertisement is
   effective?**

   Me: 1 2 3 4 5
   Partner: 1 2 3 4 5

2. **Does the analysis
   include reasons based
   on ideas in the article?**

   Me: 1 2 3 4 5
   Partner: 1 2 3 4 5

3. **Is there at least one
   Word Bank word used?**

   Me: 1 2 3 4 5
   Partner: 1 2 3 4 5

4. **Are grammar, usage,
   and mechanics correct?**

   Me: 1 2 3 4 5
   Partner: 1 2 3 4 5

Vocabulary Workshop

Add these words to your personal word bank by practicing them.

 **correspond • message • share • visual**

Define It

Complete the chart below. First, write each Word Bank word. Then, write what the word means. Finally, write what clues in the article help you figure out what the word means. Use the example as a guide.

Word	Meaning	Clues from Article
correspond	match, go together	Advertisers want ads to correspond to people watching a show.

Context clues are words that help you figure out the meaning of a word you do not know. When you are unsure about what a word means, look at the sentence that has the word. Also look at the sentences before and after the one with the word.

Show You Know

Write a comic strip in the space below. Use all the Word Bank words in a way that shows you understand their meanings.

Root Words: *vis/vid*

- A root is a word part that sets a word's main meaning. Most words that have the word part *vis* or *vid* have the meaning of the Latin word meaning "to see."

- In the list below, circle the root in each word.

visible	television
video	envision
visual	invisible
visualize	vivid
videotape	videoconference

Now choose two of the words. If you are not sure of their meanings, use a dictionary. Write a sentence for each word.

1. _____

_____

2. _____

_____

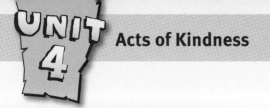

Write About It!

You have read an article about acts of kindness. Now you will write about it. Read the writing prompt. It gives your writing assignment.

Writing Prompt

After reading "Acts of Kindness," what do you know about the idea of paying it forward? Write a journal entry to tell about a time you paid it forward or a plan you have for doing this. Explain why you did or will pay it forward in this way. Use ideas from the article and at least one word from the Word Bank.

connection • dialogue • reveal • verbal

WRITING RUBRIC

In your response, you should:

- Show how you did or will pay it forward.

- Use details about the kindness movement from the article.

- Use at least one word from the Word Bank.

- Use correct grammar, usage, and mechanics.

Prewrite It

Once you are sure you understand the prompt, plan what you want to say.

1. Review your notes from the class discussion. List and organize ideas about paying it forward in the organizer.

2. Reread the article. Look for additional details to add to the first two rows.

3. In the third row, write details about what you did or will do to pay it forward. When you have filled in all the rows, go back and cross out any details you do not want to include.

What the kindness movement is:

Reasons behind the kindness movement:

How you will pay it forward and why:

Draft It

Now use your plan to draft, or write, your journal entry. The writing frame below will help you.

1. Start by explaining the kindness movement in a sentence or two.

2. Tell what you did to pay it forward (or what you will do). Explain why.

The kindness movement is _____

_____

_____

_____

I (paid /plan to pay) it forward by _____

_____

_____

_____

_____

_____

_____

_____

_____

Check It and Fix It

After you have written your journal entry, check your work. Read it aloud to be sure that it makes sense.

1. Is everything written clearly and correctly? Use the checklist on the right to see.

2. Trade your work with a classmate. Talk over ways to improve your journal entries. Use the ideas to revise your work.

3. For help with grammar, usage, and mechanics, go to the Handbook on pages 189–226.

If you have trouble putting your ideas into words, work with a partner. Tell your partner your idea. Ask the person to write it down for you. Use the person's notes to write your idea out.

✔ CHECKLIST

Evaluate your writing. A score of "5" is excellent. A score of "1" means you need to do more work. Then ask a partner to rate your work.

1. Does the journal entry describe a way you did or will pay it forward?

Me: 1 2 3 4 5
Partner: 1 2 3 4 5

2. Does the journal entry use details about the kindness movement from the article?

Me: 1 2 3 4 5
Partner: 1 2 3 4 5

3. Is there at least one Word Bank word used?

Me: 1 2 3 4 5
Partner: 1 2 3 4 5

4. Are grammar, usage, and mechanics correct?

Me: 1 2 3 4 5
Partner: 1 2 3 4 5

Vocabulary Workshop

Add these words to your personal word bank by practicing them.

WORD BANK connection • dialogue • reveal • verbal

Define It

Complete the chart below. First, write each Word Bank word. Then, write what the word means. Finally, write what the word does not mean. Use the example as a guide.

Word	What It Is	What It Is Not
connection	link between things, people, or ideas	something that separates things, people, or ideas

Show You Know

For each word from the Word Bank, write a clue sentence for a partner to see if he or she can match it with the correct word. See the example for the word *dialogue*.

- This word describes two or more people talking.

1. _____

_____

2. _____

_____

3. _____

_____

4. _____

_____

Partner Up

Have a partner figure out the words from your clues. If your partner has a hard time giving the right answer, ask him or her for advice on fixing your clue.

Word Sort

Use the chart to put the words in categories: nouns (things), verbs (actions), and adjectives (words that describe nouns). Begin with the Word Bank words. Then choose other words from the article to add to the chart.

Nouns	Verbs	Adjectives
connection dialogue		

Now that you have sorted your words, pick two from different categories and combine them into a sentence. For a challenge, pick more than two.

_____

_____

UNIT 4 Decks and Trucks

Write About It!

You have read an article about skateboarding in public places. Now you will write about it. Read the writing prompt. It gives your writing assignment.

Writing Prompt

After reading "Decks and Trucks," imagine that your community is considering setting a fine for skateboarding in public spaces. Create a flyer, in support of or against the idea, to raise public awareness of the issue. Use ideas from the article and at least one word from the Word Bank.

communication • expression • gesture • message

In your response, you should:

- Write a flyer about skateboarding in public places.

- Use details from the article to support your opinion.

- Use at least one word from the Word Bank.

- Use correct grammar, usage, and mechanics.

Prewrite It

Once you are sure you understand the prompt, plan what you want to say.

1. Review your notes from the class discussion. What do you think about skateboarding in public places? Write your opinion in the organizer. Then give reasons that explain your opinion.

2. Reread the article. Look for additional ideas that you can add to the organizer.

3. Have you supported your point of view about skateboarding in public places? Choose the ideas that best support your opinion, and circle them.

My Opinion About Skateboarding in Public Places

_____

_____

Reasons for That Opinion

_____

_____

_____

_____

_____

_____

_____

Draft It

Now use your plan to draft, or write, your flyer.
The writing frame below will help you.

1. In the first part of the headline, write yes if you think skateboarders should receive a fine for skating in public places. Write no if you believe they should not.

2. The rest of your flyer should be a list of reasons behind your opinion. Use the bullets below to organize your reasons.

If you are unsure what reasons to include, look back at your organizer. Number the ideas in order from least to most convincing. Save your most convincing argument for last in your flyer.

Fines for Skateboarding in Public Places?

The answer is _____ !

Here's why:

•

•

•

•

✔ CHECKLIST

Evaluate your writing. A score of "5" is excellent. A score of "1" means you need to do more work. Then ask a partner to rate your work.

1. **Does the flyer present a clear opinion?**

   Me: 1 2 3 4 5
   Partner: 1 2 3 4 5

2. **Does the flyer include details from the article that support the opinion?**

   Me: 1 2 3 4 5
   Partner: 1 2 3 4 5

3. **Is there at least one Word Bank word used?**

   Me: 1 2 3 4 5
   Partner: 1 2 3 4 5

4. **Are grammar, usage, and mechanics correct?**

   Me: 1 2 3 4 5
   Partner: 1 2 3 4 5

Check It and Fix It

After you have written your flyer, check your work. Look for clear reasons that prove your opinion about fines for skateboarding.

1. Is everything written clearly and correctly? Use the checklist on the right to see.

2. Trade your work with a classmate. Talk over ways to improve your flyers. Use the ideas to revise your work.

3. For help with grammar, usage, and mechanics, go to the Handbook on pages 189–226.

Vocabulary Workshop

Add these words to your personal word bank by practicing them.

communicate • expression • gesture • message

Your Choice

What other new words in the article would you like to remember? List them.

_____

_____

_____

Define It

Complete the chart below. First, write each Word Bank word. Then, write what the word means. Finally, write about a connection you have with the word. Use the example as a guide.

Word	Meaning	My Connection
communicate	to deliver some kind of message	I communicate with my friends on my social network site.

Show You Know

Write a short, short story (just a paragraph!) using the Word Bank words in the space below. Be sure your sentences show that you understand the meanings of the words.

Once upon a time _____

_____

_____

_____

_____

_____

_____

Partner Up

Ask your partner to read your story. Your partner can answer these questions: Does the story make sense? Does the story show that I know the meanings of the words?

Word Sort

Use words from the Word Bank to create new words with the endings in the chart. Then find other words in the article that you can add to each column. You can even add words that you think of or find outside the article. Examples are shown to get you started.

Words	Words with -ing	Words with -ion	Words with -ed
communicate	communicating	communication	

Now that you have sorted your words, pick two from different categories and combine them into a sentence.

_____

_____

Create a word family. In the top box, write the basic word that the Word Bank word *expression* comes from. Then add *-ing* to it.

```
┌──────────────┐
│              │
└──────────────┘
       │
┌──────────────┐
│              │
└──────────────┘
       │
┌──────────────┐
│  expression  │
└──────────────┘
```

Write About It!

You have read an article about text messaging. Now you will write about it. Read the writing prompt. It gives your writing assignment.

Writing Prompt

After reading "Check for Messages," what do you know about text messaging? Create a list of FAQs (frequently asked questions) that adults might have about text messaging. Provide answers to the questions. Use ideas from the article and at least one word from the Word Bank.

correspond • language • quote • symbolize

In your response, you should:

- Write a list of questions and answers.

- Use details from the article in your writing.

- Use at least one word from the Word Bank.

- Use correct grammar, usage, and mechanics.

Prewrite It

Once you are sure you understand the prompt, plan what you want to say.

1. Review your notes from the class discussion. Jot down important ideas about text messaging on the concept web.

2. Reread the article. Look for additional details about text messaging that you might want to include in your FAQs.

3. Look over the concept web and choose the ideas you think are most important for adults who want to understand text messaging. Circle those ideas to be sure you include them.

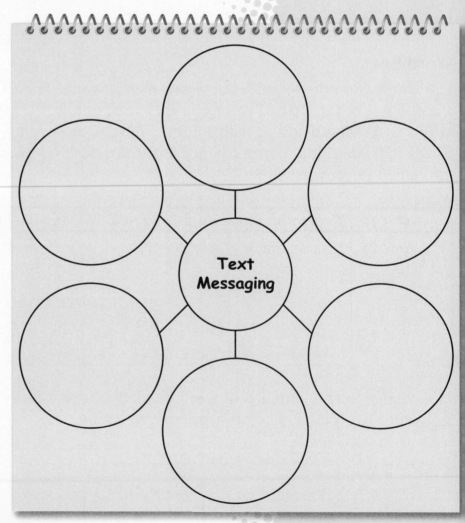

Text Messaging

Draft It

Now use your plan to draft, or write, your FAQs.
The writing frame below will help you.

1. Start by writing a question about text messaging. Then write the answer. Remember you are writing this for adults. Use appropriate language and tone.

2. Continue to write questions and answers. Think about what your audience would want to know, and use details from the article in answering the questions.

Text Messaging FAQs

Q: _____

_____

A: _____

_____

Q: _____

_____

A: _____

_____

Check It and Fix It

After you have written your FAQs, check your work. Make sure the questions and answers cover what someone new to text messaging would need to know.

1. Is everything written clearly and correctly? Use the checklist on the right to see.

2. Trade your work with a classmate. Talk over ways to improve your FAQs. Use the ideas to revise your work.

3. For help with grammar, usage, and mechanics, go to the Handbook on pages 189–226.

If you are having trouble writing the FAQs, think about your audience. Imagine that your readers know very little about text messaging and need to find out more from your writing.

✔ CHECKLIST

Evaluate your writing.
A score of "5" is excellent.
A score of "1" means you need to do more work.
Then ask a partner to rate your work.

1. Does each question include a clear answer?

Me: 1 2 3 4 5
Partner: 1 2 3 4 5

2. Do the FAQs include details about text messaging from the article?

Me: 1 2 3 4 5
Partner: 1 2 3 4 5

3. Is there at least one Word Bank word used?

Me: 1 2 3 4 5
Partner: 1 2 3 4 5

4. Are grammar, usage, and mechanics correct?

Me: 1 2 3 4 5
Partner: 1 2 3 4 5

Vocabulary Workshop

Add these words to your personal word bank by practicing them.

 **correspond • language • quote • symbolize**

Define It

In the chart below, write a synonym for each Word Bank word. Then write an antonym. Remember, synonyms have the same or almost the same meaning. Antonyms have opposite meanings. Use the example to guide your work.

Word	Synonym	Antonym
correspond	match	differ

Try using a thesaurus if you are looking for words with the same or opposite meanings. A thesaurus can help you find the exact word for your writing.

Show You Know

A dialogue is a conversation between two or more people.
Write a dialogue that uses three or more Word Bank words.
Show that you know what the Word Bank words mean.

_____ : _____
_____
_____ : _____
_____
_____ : _____
_____

Word Endings: -ation

- Adding the ending *-ation* to a verb changes the verb to a noun.

  Verb: A reporter tries to **quote** the source of information.
  Noun: Who said that famous **quotation?**

- In the chart below, write the verb that goes with each noun. An example is shown.

Noun	Verb
creation	create
starvation	
civilization	
confirmation	
cooperation	

Choose one of the nouns and one of the verbs. Write each in a sentence.

1. _____
_____

2. _____
_____

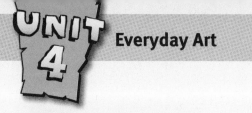

Write About It!

You have read an article about pop art. Now you will write about it. Read the writing prompt. It gives your writing assignment.

In your response, you should:

- Write an explanatory column.

- Use details from the article.

- Use at least one word from the Word Bank.

- Use correct grammar, usage, and mechanics.

Writing Prompt

After reading "Everyday Art" pick an everyday object. Write a column for an art magazine that explains why this particular object could be turned into pop art. Use ideas from the article and at least one word from the Word Bank.

connection • expression • share • visual

Prewrite It

Once you are sure you understand the prompt, plan what you want to say.

1. Review your notes from the class discussion. Begin to fill in the organizer with your ideas about an everyday object that could be a subject for pop art.

2. Reread the article. Look for additional details that you can add to the organizer. Ideas from the article will be important in the first column.

3. When you have finished working on the organizer, look it over to be sure that you have included enough ideas about turning an everyday object into art.

An object to turn into pop art: _____

Traits of pop art:	Why this object will work as pop art:

Draft It

Now use your plan to draft, or write, your art magazine column. The writing frame below will help you.

1. Start by describing the object you will turn into pop art.

2. Include details that tell why this object would make a good subject for pop art.

Looking for a new piece of pop art? I have an idea for a

perfect subject: _____

This object should be used as a subject for art because

_____

_____

_____

_____

_____

_____

_____

_____

_____

_____

Check It and Fix It

After you have written your column, check your work. Think about whether this column clearly shows why a certain object would make a good subject for pop art.

1. Is everything written clearly and correctly? Use the checklist on the right to see.

2. Trade columns with a classmate. Talk over ways to improve your columns. Use the ideas to revise your work.

3. For help with grammar, usage, and mechanics, go to the Handbook on pages 189–226.

Writing COACH

To get ideas, try using this sentence frame: I think _____ would make a good subject for pop art because _____. You can use this sentence as the basis for your column and add details.

✔ **CHECKLIST**

Evaluate your writing. A score of "5" is excellent. A score of "1" means you need to do more work. Then ask a partner to rate your work.

1. **Does the column describe an object that could be pop art?**

   Me: 1 2 3 4 5
   Partner: 1 2 3 4 5

2. **Does the column include information from the article that supports the writer's choice?**

   Me: 1 2 3 4 5
   Partner: 1 2 3 4 5

3. **Is there at least one Word Bank word used?**

   Me: 1 2 3 4 5
   Partner: 1 2 3 4 5

4. **Are grammar, usage, and mechanics correct?**

   Me: 1 2 3 4 5
   Partner: 1 2 3 4 5

Vocabulary Workshop

Add these words to your personal word bank by practicing them.

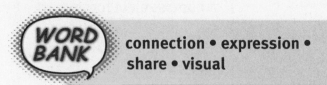

WORD BANK connection • expression • share • visual

Define It

Write a Word Bank word in each circle. Where the circles overlap, write how the paired words are the same or related. Write differences between them in the outer part of the circles.

Your Choice

What other new words in the article would you like to remember? List them.

_____

_____

_____

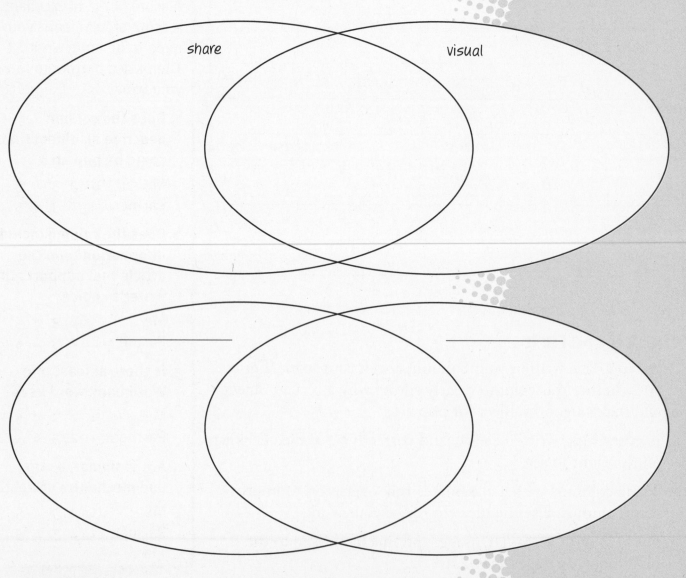

share

visual

Show You Know

Answer the questions below to show you know how each boldface Word Bank word is used.

1. To whom do you feel a strong **connection**? Why? _____

   _____

2. What would be an appropriate **expression** for anger? _____

   _____

3. Why is it sometimes difficult for young children to **share**? _____

   _____

4. Which is **visual**—a bright red sign or a loud shriek? Why? _____

   _____

Partner Up

Trade answers with a partner. Check each other's answers to see if they make sense. Are there any problems in the writing? If so, talk over how to fix them. Then make the corrections.

Word Play

In the chart below, list words that have the same or almost the same meaning as the Word Bank words.

Word Bank Words	Similar Words
connection	link, relationship
expression	
share	
visual	

Now choose two of your "new" words. Use each of them in a sentence.

1. _____

   _____

2. _____

   _____

ALL IN THE FAMILY

Create a word family. Find two forms of the word *connect* in the article.

```
connect
   |
[        ]
   |
[        ]
```

Write About It!

You have read an article about music in the movies. Now you will write about it. Read the writing prompt. It gives your writing assignment.

WRITING RUBRIC

In your response, you should:

• Identify a song to accompany a scene.

• Explain why the song is a good choice.

• Use at least one word from the Word Bank.

• Use correct grammar, usage, and mechanics.

Writing Prompt

Think of a favorite scene from a movie or a television show, or even from real life. Write a proposal that tells what song you would add to that scene and why. Use ideas from the article and at least one word from the Word Bank.

communicate • dialogue • nonverbal • visual

Prewrite It

Once you are sure you understand the prompt, plan what you want to say.

1. In the top part of the organizer, describe the scene to which you would add music.

2. In the first column, tell what feelings are part of the scene. Be specific.

3. Reread the article for information about how music can express and heighten the feelings of a scene. Jot down your ideas for music in the second column. Choose the music you like best and circle that choice.

Description of the Scene:

Feelings in the Scene:	Music That Would Work:

Draft It

Now use your plan to draft, or write, your proposal. The writing frame below will help you.

1. Start with a brief description of the scene and tell what piece of music you have chosen.

2. Then tell why you have chosen that piece of music.

The music _____ should be part of the

following scene: _____

_____

This music is best for this scene because _____

_____

_____

_____

_____

_____

_____

_____

_____

Check It and Fix It

After you have written your proposal, check your work. Imagine that you are a film maker, trying to decide, based on the reasons in the proposal, whether this piece of music is right for the scene.

1. Is everything written clearly and correctly? Use the checklist on the right to see.

2. Trade your work with a classmate. Talk over ways to improve your proposals. Use the ideas to revise your work.

3. For help with grammar, usage, and mechanics, go to the Handbook on pages 189–226.

If you have trouble choosing music, consider listening to a few pieces. What images and feelings come to your mind as you listen? Jot them down and use those ideas in your writing.

✔ **CHECKLIST**

Evaluate your writing. A score of "5" is excellent. A score of "1" means you need to do more work. Then ask a partner to rate your work.

1. Does the proposal identify a piece of music for a scene?

Me: 1 2 3 4 5
Partner: 1 2 3 4 5

2. Does the proposal explain why that piece is right for the scene?

Me: 1 2 3 4 5
Partner: 1 2 3 4 5

3. Is there at least one Word Bank word used?

Me: 1 2 3 4 5
Partner: 1 2 3 4 5

4. Are grammar, usage, and mechanics correct?

Me: 1 2 3 4 5
Partner: 1 2 3 4 5

Vocabulary Workshop

Add these words to your personal word bank by practicing them.

 **communicate • dialogue • nonverbal • visual**

Define It

Choose pairs of words from the Word Bank and write each word in a small box below. Then, in the Connection box, write how the paired words are connected. You will have to use two words twice.

| communicate | **and** | visual |

Connection:

| | **and** | |

Connection:

Show You Know

To show that you understand the words from the Word Bank, write three sentences. In each sentence, use and highlight two of the Word Bank words. (Use two of the words twice.) Use the example as a model.

- Characters in a play communicate through dialogue.

1. _____

   _____

2. _____

   _____

3. _____

   _____

Partner Up

Read your partner the sentences with the words left out. Can your partner fill in the "blanks"? If not, you might need to rewrite to make clearer sentences.

Root Words: *log/logue*

- The article word *dialogue* has a root, *logue*. The root *log* or *logue* in words usually means "word" or "thought." *Dialogue*, for example, means "the spoken words of two or more people."

- Circle the root in each word listed below.

   Catalog: a list of goods for sale

   Logical: based on facts and clear thinking

   Monologue: words spoken by one person only

   Travelogue: a piece of writing that tells about travel

Choose two of the words defined above. Explain how the root relates to the meaning. An example is shown.

- **Catalog:** A catalog is a list. A list has words.

   _____

   _____

   _____

   _____

Writing Reflection

 Do we need words to communicate well?

Look through your writing from this unit and choose the best piece. Reflect on this piece of writing by completing each sentence below.

My best piece of writing from this unit is _____

_____

I chose this piece because _____

_____

_____

While I was writing, one goal I had was _____

_____

I accomplished this goal by _____

_____

_____

This writing helped me think more about the Big Question because

_____

_____

One thing I learned while writing that can help me in the future is

_____

 How do we decide who we are?

Write About It!

You have read an article about setting goals and motivation. Now you will write about it. Read the writing prompt. It gives your writing assignment.

In your response, you should:

- Write your goal and your plan to achieve it.

- Give reasons based on the article you read.

- Use at least one word from the Word Bank.

- Use correct grammar, usage, and mechanics.

Writing Prompt

Imagine Chris Gardner has come to speak at your school. He has asked students to pick a goal they want to reach and write a four-step plan for it. You will do this too. Use ideas from the article and at least one word from the Word Bank.

conscious • expectations • ideals • individuality • presume

Prewrite It

Once you are sure you understand the prompt, plan what you want to say.

1. Review your notes from the class discussion. Jot down your goal in the Goal Plan organizer. In the Steps section, make notes of how you will achieve your goal.

2. Reread the article. Look for additional ideas to include in planning your steps. Add those to your organizer.

3. Take another look at your goal. Do you need to change it in any way after rereading the article? Read through all the steps you have listed. Which are the strongest? Cross out the ideas that are not as strong.

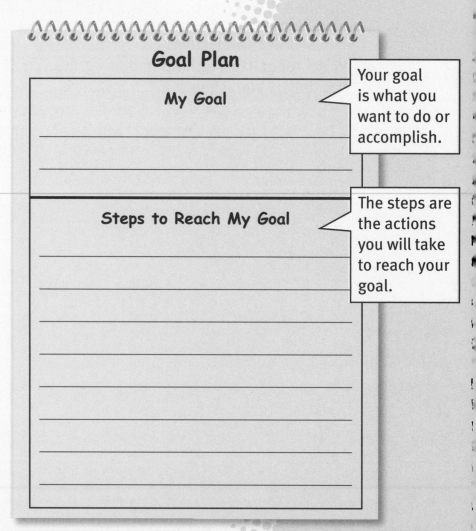

Goal Plan

My Goal

Your goal is what you want to do or accomplish.

Steps to Reach My Goal

The steps are the actions you will take to reach your goal.

Draft It

Now use your plan to draft, or write, your goal and steps. The writing frame below will help you.

1. Start by stating your goal. Finish the first line below to get started.

2. Then describe the steps you will take to reach your goal. Look at step 1 below. Complete the thought with a detailed plan. Make sure you explain your reasons with ideas from the article.

My goal is to _____

_____

• Step 1: The first thing I need to do is _____

_____

• Step 2: Next _____

_____

• Step 3: Then _____

_____

• Step 4: Finally _____

_____

Check It and Fix It

After you have written your goal plan, check your work. Try to read it with a "fresh eye." Imagine that you have never read the goal plan before.

1. Is everything written clearly and correctly? Use the checklist on the right to see.

2. Trade your work with a classmate. Talk over ways to improve your plans. Use the ideas to revise your work.

3. For help with grammar, usage, and mechanics, go to the Handbook on pages 189–226.

Writing COACH

Read a sentence to a partner. See what your partner understood from your sentence. This can help you to figure out where your writing needs to be clearer.

✔ **CHECKLIST**

Evaluate your work. A score of "5" is excellent. A score of "1" means you need to do more work. Then ask a partner to rate your work.

1. **Does the plan sound like it will help achieve the stated goal?**

   Me: 1 2 3 4 5
   Partner: 1 2 3 4 5

2. **Are there ideas from the article that explain the plan?**

   Me: 1 2 3 4 5
   Partner: 1 2 3 4 5

3. **Is there at least one Word Bank word used?**

   Me: 1 2 3 4 5
   Partner: 1 2 3 4 5

4. **Are grammar, usage, and mechanics correct?**

   Me: 1 2 3 4 5
   Partner: 1 2 3 4 5

Vocabulary Workshop

Add these words to your personal word bank by practicing them.

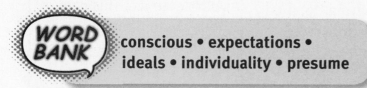

WORD BANK

conscious • expectations • ideals • individuality • presume

Define It

Choose two words from the Word Bank and write them in the small boxes below. In the "Connection" box, describe how the two words are connected. Do this for three sets of words. You will have to use one word twice.

Your Choice

What other new words in the article would you like to remember? List them.

_____

_____

_____

| ideals | and | expectations |

Connection:
Your ideals are your expectations of perfection.

| | and | |

Connection:

| | and | |

Connection:

Show You Know

Answer the questions below to show you know what each boldface Word Bank word means.

1. What is something that you are **conscious** of? _____

_____

2. What does it mean to have **expectations** of something or someone? _____

_____

3. How are **ideals** different from goals? _____

_____

4. If you **presume** something, what have you done? _____

_____

Word Endings: -ic

- By adding suffixes to words, you change their forms and meanings. The suffix -ic means "relating to" and turns a word into an adjective, a describing word. Read the example sentences below.

  Noun: Our country was founded on a democratic **ideal.**
  Adjective: Some say democracy is too **idealistic.**

  In the first sentence, **ideal** is a thing, a noun. In the second sentence, **idealistic** describes a thing, democracy. It is acting as an adjective.

- Circle the correct form of the words in parentheses.

  Everyone is a unique (individualistic, individual, individuality). We all have our own set of (idealistic, ideals) that we try to live by. It is part of what defines our (individualistic, individual, individuality). Some of us may be more (idealistic, ideals) than others, but we all create our own (individualistic, individual, individuality) lives as best we can.

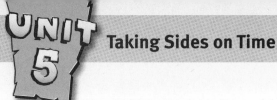
Write About It!

You have read an article about balancing your time. Now you will write about it. Read the writing prompt. It gives your writing assignment.

Writing Prompt

After reading "Taking Sides on Time," how do you think kids should balance their time? Write an advice column for your school newspaper about how people your age can manage their time. Use ideas from the article and at least one word from the Word Bank.

argument • custom • perspective • reaction • trend

WRITING RUBRIC

In your response, you should:

- Write an advice column about how people your age can manage their time.

- Give reasons for your advice based on the article you read.

- Use at least one word from the Word Bank.

- Use correct grammar, usage, and mechanics.

Prewrite It

Once you are sure you understand the prompt, plan what you want to say.

1. Review your notes from the class discussion. Give your general advice at the top. In the other sections, jot down notes about the benefits of organized activities and unstructured time.

2. Reread the article. Add information that supports or explains your advice.

3. Take another look at your advice. Do you need to change it after rereading the article? Read through your list of activities and free time. Cross out any ideas and information that are not strong.

Advice Column

My Advice

Your advice is what you think people should do to manage their time.

Activities	Free Time

This is where you list the benefits of organized activities and free time.

Draft It

Now use your plan to draft, or write, an advice column. The writing frame below will help you.

1. Start by writing down your advice. You have three choices of advice. Underline your choice.

2. Then give your support and examples. Finish the thought below by giving strong reasons for your advice. Make sure you explain your reasons with details from the article.

THIS JUST IN

How to Manage Your Time

I think it is (important, challenging, impossible) to manage

your time from day to day. Deciding what to do and when

to do it is _____

_____

_____

_____

_____

_____

_____

Check It and Fix It

After you have written your advice column, check your work. Try to read it with a "fresh eye." Imagine that you have never read the advice column before.

1. Is everything written clearly and correctly? Use the checklist on the right to see.

2. Exchange work with a classmate. Talk over ways to improve your advice columns. Use the ideas to revise your work.

3. For help with grammar, usage, and mechanics, go to the Handbook on pages 189–226.

✔ CHECKLIST

Evaluate your work. A score of "5" is excellent. A score of "1" means you need to do more work. Then ask a partner to rate your work.

1. Does the column present advice clearly?

Me: 1 2 3 4 5
Partner: 1 2 3 4 5

2. Are there ideas from the article that support the advice?

Me: 1 2 3 4 5
Partner: 1 2 3 4 5

3. Is there at least one Word Bank word used?

Me: 1 2 3 4 5
Partner: 1 2 3 4 5

4. Are grammar, usage, and mechanics correct?

Me: 1 2 3 4 5
Partner: 1 2 3 4 5

Vocabulary Workshop

Add these words to your personal word bank by practicing them.

 **WORD BANK** argument • custom • perspective • reaction • trend

Your Choice

What other new words in the article would you like to remember? List them.

_____

_____

_____

Define It

Choose two words from the Word Bank and write them on either side of the triangle below. Then describe how the two words are connected by completing the "because" portion of the sentence. Do this for three sets of words. You will have to use one word twice.

custom   **is connected to**   trend

_____   _____

because _____

_____

is connected to

_____   _____

because _____

_____

is connected to

_____   _____

because _____

_____

Show You Know

Write a comic strip in the space below using all of the Word Bank words in a way that shows you understand the words.

Word Play

Using exact words in your writing can make what you have to say more lively, interesting, and detailed. In the chart below, list some additional words that mean the same or about the same as the Word Bank words. Think of words that give a precise meaning. Examples are shown.

Word Bank Words	Similar Words
argument	disagreement, debate
custom	
reaction	

Now try out some of the words to see how they can make your writing more interesting. Rewrite each of the sentences, substituting one of your words for the boldface word.

1. I do not want to get into an **argument** about it. _____

_____

2. Does your family have any holiday **customs**? _____

_____

3. Did you see her **reaction** when she realized she had won?

_____

ALL IN THE FAMILY

Knowing the root of a word can help you understand variations of the word. Find two variations of the root word *custom* and write them in the boxes below.

custom

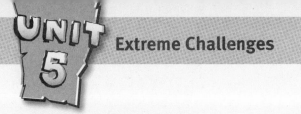

Write About It!

You have read an article about extreme sports and the people who do them. Now you will write about it. Read the writing prompt. It gives your writing assignment.

WRITING RUBRIC

In your response, you should:

- Write a job description for an extreme athlete.

- Provide details based on the article you read.

- Use at least one word from the Word Bank.

- Use correct grammar, usage, and mechanics.

Writing Prompt

Write a job description for an extreme athlete, explaining what the job entails, the requirements, and the qualifications. Use ideas from the article and at least one word from the Word Bank.

appearance • calculate • logical • personality • respond

Prewrite It

Once you are sure you understand the prompt, plan what you want to say.

1. Review your notes from the class discussion. What characteristics should an extreme athlete have? How would you describe the job? Use the organizer to make notes for your job description.

2. Reread the article. Look for more ideas to add to your organizer.

3. Take another look at your organizer. Group any similar characteristics or qualifications together to help organize your thoughts. Cross out any repetitive ideas.

Extreme Athlete Job

What the Job Entails

This is where you describe the actual job.

Qualifications and Characteristics

This is where you describe the type of person you are looking for to fill the job.

Draft It

Now use your plan to draft, or write, your job description. The writing frame below will help you.

1. Start by describing the type of person you are looking to fill the job. You have three choices. Underline your choice.

2. Then give details about the characteristics you are looking for in an extreme athlete by finishing the thought below. Make sure you include ideas from the article in the job description.

Read a sentence to a partner. See what your partner understood from your sentence. This can help you to figure out where your writing needs to be clearer.

THIS JUST IN

Extreme Athlete Needed

We are looking for a (fearless, smart, wild) athlete to compete in extreme sports competitions. We participate in weekly competitions around the country, and we need someone who _____

_____

_____

_____

_____

_____

Check It and Fix It

After you have written your job description, check your work. Imagine you do not know anything about extreme athletes. Look to see if the description gives enough details.

1. Is everything written clearly and correctly? Use the checklist on the right to see.

2. Trade your work with a classmate. Talk over ways to improve your job descriptions. Use the ideas to revise your work.

3. For help with grammar, usage, and mechanics, go to the Handbook on pages 189–226.

✔ CHECKLIST

Evaluate your work.
A score of "5" is excellent.
A score of "1" means you need to do more work.
Then ask a partner to rate your work.

1. Is the job description clearly written?

Me: 1 2 3 4 5
Partner: 1 2 3 4 5

2. Are there ideas from the article that explain the job requirements?

Me: 1 2 3 4 5
Partner: 1 2 3 4 5

3. Is there at least one Word Bank word used?

Me: 1 2 3 4 5
Partner: 1 2 3 4 5

4. Are grammar, usage, and mechanics correct?

Me: 1 2 3 4 5
Partner: 1 2 3 4 5

Vocabulary Workshop

Add these words to your personal word bank by practicing them.

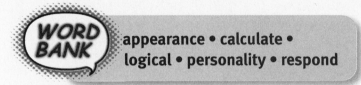

WORD BANK appearance • calculate • logical • personality • respond

Define It

Complete the chart below. First, tell what the Word Bank word means. Then write the context clues from the article that help you understand the word's meaning. Remember that context clues are words or phrases around the word you don't know. The context words can give you clues to the difficult word's meaning.

Word	Meaning	Context Clues
appearance	the way something or someone looks	"Eleven feet is almost the height of a one-story building."

Your Choice

What other new words in the article would you like to remember? List them.

_____

_____

_____

When looking for context clues, certain key words can help you to understand the word you do not know. Words like *is, was, or, such as,* and *means* often point you to the meaning of the word you are having trouble with.

Show You Know

For each word from the Word Bank, write a clue sentence for a partner to see if he or she can match it with the correct word. See the example below for the word *respond*.

- When someone asks you a question, you usually do this.

1. _____

   _____

2. _____

   _____

3. _____

   _____

Partner Up

Trade your sentences with a partner. Check each other's answers to make sure you both got them right.

Word Sort

Sort the Word Bank words by category, using the boxes below. Read through the article and find additional words you can add to each box. Examples are shown.

Nouns	Verbs	Adjectives
appearance		logical

Now that you have sorted your words, pick two from different categories and combine them into a sentence. For a challenge, pick more than two to use in a sentence.

1. _____

   _____

2. _____

   _____

ALL IN THE FAMILY

Knowing the root of a word can help you understand variations of the word. Find two variations of the root word *person* and write them in the boxes below.

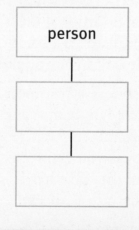

person

UNIT 5

The Creative Connection

WRITING RUBRIC

In your response, you should:

- Write a creative solution to an everyday problem.

- Provide details based on the article you read.

- Use at least one word from the Word Bank.

- Use correct grammar, usage, and mechanics.

Write About It!

You have read an article about creative thinking. Now you will write about it. Read the writing prompt. It gives your writing assignment.

Writing Prompt

Imagine your teacher has posted a flyer for a creative thinking contest at your school. You have to come up with a creative solution for a problem you encounter in your daily life. Use ideas from the article and at least one word from the Word Bank.

discover • diverse • reflect • similar • unique

Prewrite It

Once you are sure you understand the prompt, plan what you want to say.

1. Review your notes from the class discussion. Use the organizer to make notes on common problems that need a solution. Then brainstorm ideas for how to creatively solve the problem.

2. Reread the article. Look for additional ideas to help brainstorm a solution. Add those to your organizer.

3. Choose a common problem from your organizer. Are there more ideas you can think of that might solve it? If so, add them to your list.

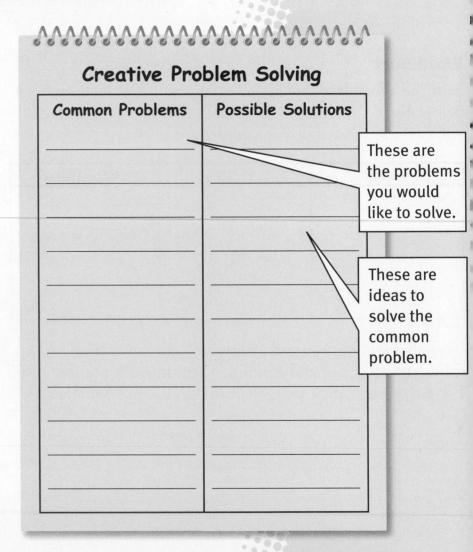

Creative Problem Solving

Common Problems	Possible Solutions

These are the problems you would like to solve.

These are ideas to solve the common problem.

Draft It

Now use your plan to draft, or write, your creative solution. The writing frame below will help you.

1. Start by describing the problem you are going to solve. Use the first sentence as a way to get started.

2. Then give the details on how your solution will work. Read the second sentence below and finish the thought. Make sure you include ideas from the article in the solution.

A Creative Solution

We have all encountered a situation like this: _____

_____

_____

One solution to this problem is _____

_____

_____

_____

_____

_____

_____

_____

Check It and Fix It

After you have written your creative solution, check your work. As you read, imagine yourself encountering this problem and using your method to solve it. Would your solution work?

1. Is everything written clearly and correctly? Use the checklist on the right to see.

2. Exchange work with a classmate. Talk over ways you both might improve your solutions. Use the ideas to revise your work.

3. For help with grammar, usage, and mechanics, go to the Handbook on pages 189–226.

✔ **CHECKLIST**

Evaluate your work. A score of "5" is excellent. A score of "1" means you need to do more work. Then ask a partner to rate your work.

1. **Does the creative solution make sense?**

   Me: 1 2 3 4 5
   Partner: 1 2 3 4 5

2. **Are there ideas from the article that support the solution?**

   Me: 1 2 3 4 5
   Partner: 1 2 3 4 5

3. **Is there at least one Word Bank word used?**

   Me: 1 2 3 4 5
   Partner: 1 2 3 4 5

4. **Are grammar, usage, and mechanics correct?**

   Me: 1 2 3 4 5
   Partner: 1 2 3 4 5

Vocabulary Workshop

Add these words to your personal word bank by practicing them.

 **WORD BANK** discover • diverse • reflect • similar • unique

Your Choice

What other new words in the article would you like to remember? List them.

_____

_____

_____

Define It

Choose two words from the Word Bank and write them in the Venn diagram circles below. Where the circles intersect, describe how the two words could be connected. Do this for three sets of words. You will have to use one word twice.

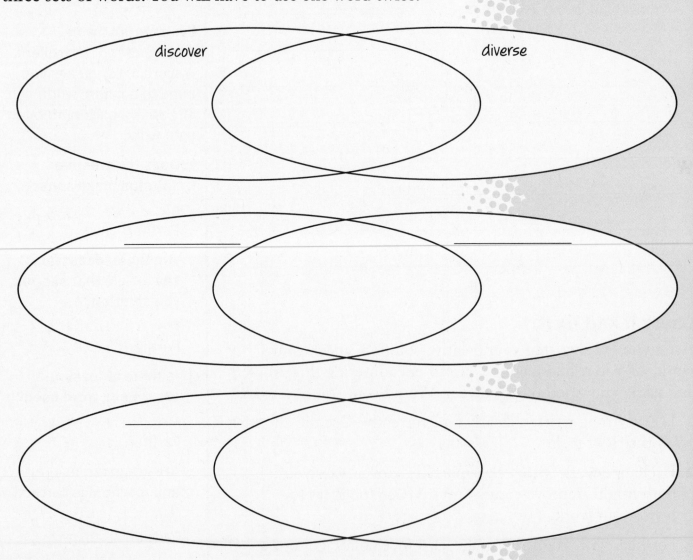

discover   diverse

Show You Know

In the space below, write a short, short story (just one paragraph!) using the Word Bank words. Be sure your sentences show that you understand the meanings of the words. Make sure to use all Word Bank words at least once. Completing the sentence below should get you started.

Sometimes when you least expect it _____

_____

_____

_____

_____

_____

_____

Partner Up

Trade stories with a partner. Check each other's writing to see if the story makes sense. Are there any problems in the writing that need to be fixed? If so, talk over how to fix them. Then make the corrections.

Word Endings: *-ities* / *-ity*

- When you add the word ending *-ities* / *-ity* to an adjective, you change the word from a descriptor to a thing, or noun.

    Adjective: These two sweaters are very **similar.**

    Noun: Notice the **similarities** between these two sweaters.

- Circle the correct form of the words in parentheses.

    (Diverse, Diversity) people and opinions are at the heart of public debate. People who share (similar, similarities) in their thoughts will usually have (similar, similarities) opinions about things. Those with (diverse, diversity) opinions can also share (similar, similarities) ideas. The (diverse, diversity) of ideas and opinions we hear in public debates helps inform all of us.

Writing Reflection

 ## How do we decide who we are?

Look through your writing from this unit and choose the best piece. Reflect on this piece of writing by completing each sentence below.

My best piece of writing from this unit is _____

_____

I chose this piece because _____

_____

_____

While I was writing, one goal I had was _____

_____

I accomplished this goal by _____

_____

_____

This writing helped me think more about the Big Question because

_____

_____

One thing I learned while writing that can help me in the future is

_____

UNIT 6

 How much do our communities shape us?

In your response, you should:

- Write an informational flyer.

- Explain why volunteering is good for you.

- Use at least one word from the Word Bank.

- Use correct grammar, usage, and mechanics.

Write About It!

You have read an article about how helping others can make you feel better. Now you will write about it. Read the writing prompt. It gives your writing assignment.

Writing Prompt

After reading "Help You, Help Me," what do you see as benefits of volunteering? Write a flyer to recruit new volunteers to a community center. Explain why volunteering is good for you. Use ideas from the article and at least one word from the Word Bank.

community • family • order • survey • values

Prewrite It

Once you are sure you understand the prompt, plan what you want to say.

1. Review your notes from the class discussion. In the web, write reasons that volunteering is good for people.

2. Reread the article. Look for additional details about why volunteering is good for the people doing the volunteering.

3. Your flyer is supposed to tell people why it would be good for them to volunteer. Look in your web for the most convincing arguments. Circle those in your web so that you are sure to use them in your writing.

Draft It

Now use your plan to draft, or write, your flyer. The writing frame below will help you.

1. Your flyer will start with a statement about volunteering.

2. The rest of your flyer will have details that support the main idea about volunteering. Think about the tone and language of the flyer. What will get people excited about volunteering?

Want to make a difference?

Our community center needs you! Volunteering is good for you. Here are just a few reasons:

-
-
-
-
-

Check It and Fix It

After you have written your flyer, check your work. Read it aloud with a partner to see if it sounds convincing and friendly.

1. Is everything written clearly and correctly? Use the checklist on the right to see.

2. Trade your work with a classmate. Talk over ways you both might improve your flyers. Use the ideas to revise your work.

3. For help with grammar, usage, and mechanics, go to the Handbook on pages 189–226.

Persuasive writing uses language that makes readers think a certain way or do a certain thing. The best way to persuade readers is to state an opinion and support that opinion with facts.

✔ CHECKLIST

Evaluate your writing. A score of "5" is excellent. A score of "1" means you need to do more work. Then ask a partner to rate your work.

1. **Does the flyer use persuasive language?**

   Me: 1 2 3 4 5
   Partner: 1 2 3 4 5

2. **Does the flyer include details about volunteering from the article?**

   Me: 1 2 3 4 5
   Partner: 1 2 3 4 5

3. **Is there at least one Word Bank word used?**

   Me: 1 2 3 4 5
   Partner: 1 2 3 4 5

4. **Are grammar, usage, and mechanics correct?**

   Me: 1 2 3 4 5
   Partner: 1 2 3 4 5

Vocabulary Workshop

Add these words to your personal word bank by practicing them.

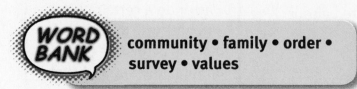

WORD BANK community • family • order • survey • values

Your Choice

What other new words in the article would you like to remember? List them.

_____

_____

_____

Define It

Complete the chart below. First, give a real-life example of the Word Bank word. Then, tell your connection to the word. Use the example as a guide.

Word	Meaning	Connection
community	a group of people who live in the same area	I am part of a community in my town, my family, and my school.

Show You Know

To show that you understand the Word Bank words, write three sentences. In each sentence, use and highlight two of the words. Use one of the words twice. Use the example as a model.

- A family is a certain kind of community.

1. _____

   _____

2. _____

   _____

3. _____

   _____

Partner Up

Trade sentences with a partner. Check to see if the sentences make sense. If not, suggest ways to fix them.

Word Play

Using exact words in your writing can make what you say more lively, interesting, and detailed. In the chart below, list some additional words that mean the same or about the same as the Word Bank words. Think of words that give a precise meaning. Examples are shown.

Word Bank Words	Similar Words
community	group, society
order	
values	

Now try out some of the words to see how they can make your writing more precise. Write a sentence using a new word for *order* and *values*.

1. _____

   _____

2. _____

   _____

ALL IN THE FAMILY

Did you notice these forms of *family* in the article? Family has other forms too. They belong to the same word *family*.

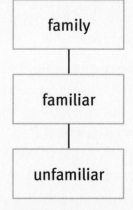

family

familiar

unfamiliar

UNIT 6

Making Everyone Welcome

WRITING RUBRIC

Write About It!

You have read an article about no-kill animal shelters. Now you will write about it. Read the writing prompt. It gives your writing assignment.

Writing Prompt

Your community has just started a blog asking citizens whether or not money should be spent to make the area more accessible to people with disabilities. Write a post with your opinion. Use ideas from the article and at least one word from the Word Bank.

form • group • involve • isolate • participation

Prewrite It

Once you are sure you understand the prompt, plan what you want to say.

1. Review your notes from the class discussion. Jot down your thoughts in the organizer.

2. Reread the article. Look for additional details about the costs and benefits of making communities accessible for people with disabilities.

3. You are writing a blog entry that gives your opinion. Look at the organizer and decide which side you will write about. Find and circle the strongest facts on that side of the organizer.

Making Communities Accessible

Benefits	Costs

Draft It

Now use your plan to write your blog entry. The writing frame below will help you.

1. Your blog entry should start with your main idea. Circle which statement best expresses your thought.

2. Continue the blog by writing reasons that support your opinion.

Our community (should, should not) spend extra

money to make our community accessible to

people with disabilities. The reasons for my

opinion are: _____

_____

_____

_____

_____

_____

_____

_____

Check It and Fix It

After you have written your blog entry, check your work. Read with a "fresh eye" to make sure it makes sense and to look for mistakes.

1. Is everything written clearly and correctly? Use the checklist on the right to see.

2. Trade your work with a classmate. Talk over ways to improve the blog entries. Use the ideas to revise your work.

3. For help with grammar, usage, and mechanics, go to the Handbook on pages 189–226.

A blog entry is written in your own "voice." Read the blog entry aloud to hear if it sounds natural. If not, say your thoughts and ask a partner to write them as you speak.

✔ CHECKLIST

Evaluate your writing. A score of "5" is excellent. A score of "1" means you need to do more work. Then ask a partner to rate your work.

1. **Does the blog state an opinion about making the community accessible for those with disabilities?**

   Me: 1 2 3 4 5
   Partner: 1 2 3 4 5

2. **Does the writing include information about accessibility from the article?**

   Me: 1 2 3 4 5
   Partner: 1 2 3 4 5

3. **Is there at least one Word Bank word used?**

   Me: 1 2 3 4 5
   Partner: 1 2 3 4 5

4. **Are grammar, usage, and mechanics correct?**

   Me: 1 2 3 4 5
   Partner: 1 2 3 4 5

Vocabulary Workshop

Add these words to your personal word bank by practicing them.

 **WORD BANK**   form • group • involve • isolate • participation

Your Choice

What other new words in the article would you like to remember? List them.

_____

_____

_____

Define It

Look at each pair of Word Bank words. Explain how the two words might be connected. For example, how could *group* and *isolate* be connected? You might feel *isolated* if you are not part of a certain *group*.

form	**and**	group

Connection:

involve	**and**	participation

Connection:

isolate	**and**	form

Connection:

Show You Know

For two words from the Word Bank, write a clue sentence for a partner to see if he or she can match it with the correct term. Use the example below for the word *isolated*.

- This is something that happens when you are alone.

1. _____

   _____

2. _____

   _____

Partner Up

Trade your answers with a partner. Check each other's answers to see if they make sense. Are there any problems in the writing that need to be fixed? If so, talk over how to fix them. Then make the corrections.

Word Endings: -ment

- When you add the ending *-ment* to a verb, you change the verb into a noun. The most common meaning when you add *-ment* is "an act of doing something."

  Verb: I **involve** myself in service with my student council.
  Noun: This **involvement** helps me as much as it helps other people.

- Add *-ment* to each verb to make a noun. Look for spelling changes!

Verb	Noun
argue	
establish	
govern	

Choose two of the nouns and use each of them in a sentence.

1. _____

   _____

2. _____

   _____

ALL IN THE FAMILY

Look through the article to find two other words in the same word family as *participate*.

participate

Write About It!

You have read an article about mentoring in communities. Now you will write about it. Read the writing prompt. It gives your writing assignment.

Writing Prompt

Write a job description for a mentor. Include details for what makes a good mentor and why someone would want to be a mentor. Use ideas from the article and at least one word from the Word Bank.

generation • influence • involve • judge • support

WRITING RUBRIC

In your response, you should:

• Describe a mentor's characteristics.

• Use the article's details in the job description.

• Use at least one word from the Word Bank.

• Use correct grammar, usage, and mechanics.

Prewrite It

Once you are sure you understand the prompt, plan what you want to write.

1. Review your notes from the class discussion. Think about the most important points of being a good mentor. Begin to list your ideas in the organizer.

2. Reread the article. Look for additional details to add to the organizer.

3. Look back at the organizer. Think about which ideas about mentoring are the most important. These are the ideas you will want to include in your writing. Cross out the rest.

Mentors

What They Do	What They Are Like

Draft It

Now use your plan to draft, or write, your job description. The writing frame below will help you.

1. Start by explaining the requirements of the job. What do mentors do?

2. List the job requirements for mentors. What personal characteristics and training do they need?

If you have trouble putting your ideas into words, work with a partner. Tell your partner what you want to say. Ask the person to write it down for you. Use the person's notes to write.

■■■ **THIS JUST IN** ■■■

Help Wanted: Mentor

Mentors will be doing the following on the job:

-

-

-

Successful candidates will have the following

qualifications:

-

-

-

✔ **CHECKLIST**

Evaluate your writing. A score of "5" is excellent. A score of "1" means you need to do more work. Then ask a partner to rate your work.

1. Does the description explain the job of being a mentor along with the job requirements?

Me: 1 2 3 4 5
Partner: 1 2 3 4 5

2. Are there ideas from the article in the description?

Me: 1 2 3 4 5
Partner: 1 2 3 4 5

3. Is there at least one Word Bank word used?

Me: 1 2 3 4 5
Partner: 1 2 3 4 5

4. Are grammar, usage, and mechanics correct?

Me: 1 2 3 4 5
Partner: 1 2 3 4 5

Check It and Fix It

After you have written your job description, check your work. Be sure that it explains the job of being a mentor.

1. Is everything written clearly and correctly? Use the checklist on the right to see.

2. Trade your work with a classmate. Talk over ways to improve your job descriptions. Use the ideas to revise your work.

3. For help with grammar, usage, and mechanics, go to the Handbook on pages 189–226.

Vocabulary Workshop

Add these words to your personal word bank by practicing them.

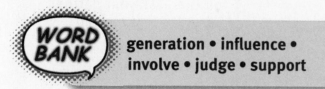

WORD BANK generation • influence • involve • judge • support

Define It

Complete the chart below. Write each Word Bank word in the chart. Tell what each word means. Then tell what the words do not mean. Use the example as a guide.

Word	What It Is	What It Is Not
generation	a group defined by age	a group defined by where people live

Show You Know

For three words from the Word Bank, write a clue sentence for a partner to see if he or she can match it with the correct term. See the example for the word *support*.

- This word describes something you might offer to help someone.

1. _____

   _____

2. _____

   _____

3. _____

   _____

Partner Up

Have a partner figure out the words from your clues. If your partner has a hard time, ask for advice to make your clues easier to answer.

Word Endings: *-ial, -ive*

- Adding *-ive* to a noun or verb changes the word into an adjective.

  Verb: As a coach, Ms. Turner knows how to **support** team members.
  Adjective: Her **supportive** attitude helps us win games!

- Adding *-ial* to a verb changes the verb into an adjective.

  Verb: What kinds of music **influence** your playing?
  Adjective: Rock rhythms are **influential** in my drumming.

- Circle the correct form of the word in parentheses.

  I turn to my mother for (support, supportive) when I need help. She is very (support, supportive), especially when it comes to my writing. She always has great ideas! Some people say that famous authors (influence, influential) them. I am lucky to have an (influence, influential) person right in my own home!

Find two words in the article with the word ending *-ment*. Write the verb and the noun form of the word.

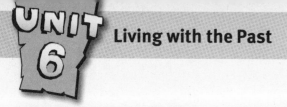 **Living with the Past**

Write About It!

You have read an article about communities and their identities. Now you will write about it. Read the writing prompt. It gives your writing assignment.

Writing Prompt

After reading "Living with the Past," consider how things that happen in communities affect people who live there. Write a travel brochure for a community with a past. Use ideas from the article and at least one word from the Word Bank.

belief • body • common • history • pattern

Prewrite It

Once you are sure you understand the prompt, plan what you want to write.

1. Review your notes from the class discussion. Choose a community with an interesting past as the basis for your work. You can choose one from the article or one that you found through research.

2. Reread the article. Look for details to add to your organizer.

3. If needed, use print or Internet sources to research a community. Add those details to your organizer to use in your brochure.

Community: _____

Facts about the community's past	Why would people want to visit?

Draft It

Now use your plan to draft, or write, your travel brochure. The writing frame below will help you.

1. Start by giving the name of the community. Then tell a little bit about the community and why it is famous.

2. Give reasons that people would want to visit. A travel brochure should get people excited about visiting a place.

Organize your reasons to leave a good impression. Put the best reason for visiting the community last in your list of reasons.

Come visit _____ !

What makes this community famous? _____

_____

_____

_____

Why should you visit? _____

_____

_____

_____

_____

✔ CHECKLIST

Evaluate your writing. A score of "5" is excellent. A score of "1" means you need to do more work. Then ask a partner to rate your work.

1. **Does the brochure give good reasons that people would want to visit the community?**

   Me: 1 2 3 4 5
   Partner: 1 2 3 4 5

2. **Does the writing include information from the article or from reliable research?**

   Me: 1 2 3 4 5
   Partner: 1 2 3 4 5

3. **Is there at least one Word Bank word used?**

   Me: 1 2 3 4 5
   Partner: 1 2 3 4 5

4. **Are grammar, usage, and mechanics correct?**

   Me: 1 2 3 4 5
   Partner: 1 2 3 4 5

Check It and Fix It

After you have written your travel brochure, check over your work. Read it as if you are trying to decide whether you should plan a trip to a certain community.

1. Is everything written clearly and correctly? Use the checklist on the right to see.

2. Trade your work with a classmate. Talk over ways you both might improve your brochures. Use the ideas to revise your work.

3. For help with grammar, usage, and mechanics, go to the Handbook on pages 189–226.

Vocabulary Workshop

Add these words to your personal word bank by practicing them.

WORD BANK

belief • body • common • history • pattern

Define It

Complete the chart below. First, tell what the Word Bank word means. Then tell what clues in the article help you figure out what the word means. Use the example as a guide.

Word	Meaning	Clues from Article
belief	an important idea	Viewers and visitors in Punxsutawney all have the same idea about one thing.

Your Choice

What other new words in the article would you like to remember? List them.

_____

_____

_____

Word COACH

Context clues are words that help you figure out a word you don't know. When you aren't sure about what a word means, look in the sentence with the word. Look at the sentences before and after the word.

Show You Know

Write a comic strip in the space below. Use all the Word Bank words in a way that shows you understand their meanings.

Word Sort

Sort words from the article. Use the boxes below to sort nouns, verbs, and adjectives. Start with words from the Word Bank. Then look through the article for other words.

Nouns	Verbs	Adjectives
belief		common

Now that you have sorted your words, pick two from different categories and combine them into a sentence. For a challenge, pick more than two.

1. _____

_____

2. _____

_____

Find two other words in the article in the same word family as *belief*.

belief

Write About It!

You have read an article about what causes people to want to succeed. Now you will write about it. Read the writing prompt. It gives your writing assignment.

Writing Prompt

Write a dialogue between yourself and a friend on what should motivate teens. Focus on whether or not communities should pay kids to succeed. Use ideas from the article and at least one word from the Word Bank.

belief • connection • participation • prepare • support

In your response, you should:

- Write a dialogue between two people.

- Use details from the article in your writing.

- Use at least one word from the Word Bank.

- Use correct grammar, usage, and mechanics.

Prewrite It

Once you are sure you understand the prompt, plan what you want to say.

1. Review your notes from the class discussion. Use the organizer to jot down ideas both in favor of and against paying kids to succeed.

2. Reread the article. Look for additional details to support both sides. Add those ideas to the organizer.

3. Decide how to write your dialogue. Will you take one side and your friend take the other? Or will you simply be discussing the ideas? Circle the details in the organizer that you would like to include.

Should communities pay kids to succeed?

Yes, they should, because:	No, they should not, because:

Draft It

Now use your plan to draft, or write, your dialogue.
The writing frame below will help you.

1. Dialogue is the words of each speaker. Who will speak first? Write the person's name on the line and follow with the dialogue.

2. Continue the form to write the dialogue.

_____ : _____
                     _____

_____ : _____
                     _____

_____ : _____
                     _____

_____ : _____
                     _____

_____ : _____
                     _____

_____ : _____
                     _____

Check It and Fix It

After you have written your dialogue, check your work.
Read it aloud with a friend to see if it sounds like natural speech.

1. Is everything written clearly and correctly? Use the checklist on the right to see.

2. Trade your work with a classmate. Talk over ways you both might improve your dialogues. Use the ideas to revise your work.

3. For help with grammar, usage, and mechanics, go to the Handbook on pages 189–226.

Writing COACH

Dialogue should sound like two people talking. Listen to people around you talking before you write. Read your dialogue aloud to see if it sounds natural or if it sounds "stiff."

✔ **CHECKLIST**

Evaluate your writing. A score of "5" is excellent. A score of "1" means you need to do more work. Then ask a partner to rate your work.

1. Does the dialogue sound like people really speak?

Me: 1 2 3 4 5
Partner: 1 2 3 4 5

2. Does the writing include information about paying teens to succeed from the article?

Me: 1 2 3 4 5
Partner: 1 2 3 4 5

3. Is there at least one Word Bank word used?

Me: 1 2 3 4 5
Partner: 1 2 3 4 5

4. Are grammar, usage, and mechanics correct?

Me: 1 2 3 4 5
Partner: 1 2 3 4 5

Vocabulary Workshop

Add these words to your personal word bank by practicing them.

 **WORD BANK** belief • connection • participation • prepare • support

Define It

In the chart below, write a synonym for each Word Bank word. Then write an antonym. Remember, synonyms mean the same or almost the same thing. Antonyms have opposite meanings. Use the example to guide your work.

Word	Synonym	Antonym
belief	idea	doubt

Your Choice

What other new words in the article would you like to remember? List them.

_____

_____

_____

 **Word COACH**

Try using a thesaurus if you are looking for words with the same or opposite meanings. A thesaurus can help you find a word to make your writing precise.

Show You Know

A dialogue is a conversation between two or more people. Write a dialogue that uses three of the Word Bank words. Show that you know what the Word Bank words mean.

_____ : _____

_____

_____ : _____

_____

_____ : _____

_____

Partner Up

Trade your answers with a partner. Check each other's answers to see if they make sense. Are there any problems in the writing that need to be fixed? If so, talk over how to fix them. Then make the corrections.

Word Sort

Sort words from the article. Use the boxes below to sort nouns, verbs, and adjectives. Start with words from the Word Bank. Then look through the article to find other words to add.

Nouns	Verbs	Adjectives
connection	prepare	

Now that you have sorted your words, pick two from different categories and combine them into a sentence. For a challenge, pick more than two.

1. _____

_____

2. _____

_____

Add -ive to the word support. Label which is a verb and which is an adjective.

support

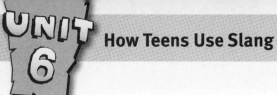

Unit 6 — How Teens Use Slang

Write About It!

You have read an article about slang. Now you will write about it. Read the writing prompt. It gives your writing assignment.

Writing Prompt

After reading "How Teens Use Slang," how do you think slang can bring people together—or keep them apart? Create a slang dictionary. Use ideas from the article and at least one word from the Word Bank.

community • culture • figure • group • isolate

Prewrite It

Once you are sure you understand the prompt, plan what you want to say.

1. Review your notes from the class discussion. Include a few important ideas about slang for a one-sentence introduction to your dictionary.

2. Start listing your slang terms. For each one, include a short definition.

3. You will need to include each word's part of speech. To do this, think about each word's job. Ask yourself: Is this word an action, a thing, or a describer? Look at parts of speech in your Word Banks and in dictionaries to figure out the parts of speech of your words.

Why slang is important/why people use slang:

_____

_____

Word	Part of Speech	Meaning
_____	_____	_____
_____	_____	_____
_____	_____	_____
_____	_____	_____
_____	_____	_____
_____	_____	_____
_____	_____	_____

Draft It

Now use your plan to draft, or write, your dictionary of slang. The writing frame below will help you.

1. Start with a one-sentence introduction using ideas from the article. Complete the sentence in the writing frame.

2. Make your dictionary like a real dictionary. Each entry includes the word, with its part of speech and definition.

Say the words aloud to be sure that you have written them correctly. Try out the meanings by creating sentences with the slang words.

Slang Dictionary

Slang is important because _____

_____

_____

(word)   (part of speech)   (meaning)

_____   _____   : _____

_____   _____   : _____

_____   _____   : _____

_____   _____   : _____

_____   _____   : _____

_____   _____   : _____

_____   _____   : _____

Check It and Fix It

After you have written your dictionary, check your work. Imagine you have never heard these words before. Will your dictionary help someone who is unfamiliar with slang?

1. Is everything written clearly and correctly? Use the checklist on the right to see.

2. Trade your work with a classmate. Talk over ways you both might improve your dictionaries. Use the ideas to revise your work.

3. For help with grammar, usage, and mechanics, go to the Handbook on pages 189–226.

✔ CHECKLIST

Evaluate your writing. A score of "5" is excellent. A score of "1" means you need to do more work. Then ask a partner to rate your work.

1. **Does the dictionary's introduction use ideas from the article?**

   Me: 1 2 3 4 5
   Partner: 1 2 3 4 5

2. **Are parts of speech and meanings in the dictionary?**

   Me: 1 2 3 4 5
   Partner: 1 2 3 4 5

3. **Is there at least one Word Bank word used?**

   Me: 1 2 3 4 5
   Partner: 1 2 3 4 5

4. **Are grammar, usage, and mechanics correct?**

   Me: 1 2 3 4 5
   Partner: 1 2 3 4 5

Vocabulary Workshop

Add these words to your personal word bank by practicing them.

 **community • culture • figure • group • isolate**

Define It

Complete the chart below. First, give a real-life example of the Word Bank word. Then, tell your connection to the word. Use the example as a guide.

Word	Real-Life Example	Connection
culture	We study cultures in social studies.	I wrote a report about a culture in South America.

Show You Know

Write a short, short story (just a paragraph!) using the Word Bank words in the space below. Be sure your sentences show that you understand the meanings of the words.

Once upon a time _____

_____

_____

_____

_____

_____

Partner Up

Ask a partner to read your story. Does the story make sense? If not, your partner can suggest ways to fix it.

Word Sort

Use words from the Word Bank to create new words with the endings in the chart. Then find other words in the article that you can add to each column by adding new endings. You can even add words that you think of or find on your own. Examples are shown to get you started.

Words with *-ing*	Words with *-ion*	Words with *-ed*
grouping	isolation	

Now that you have sorted your words, pick two from different categories and combine them into a sentence. For a challenge, pick more than two.

1. _____

_____

2. _____

_____

Create a word family. Add *-ing* and *-ion* to the Word Bank word *isolate*.

isolate

UNIT 6 Buying Power

Write About It!

You have read an article about how advertising affects teens. Now you will write about it. Read the writing prompt. It gives your writing assignment.

Writing Prompt

After reading "Buying Power," what do you think about the way that advertising affects teens? Write an advice column for your school newspaper on what teens should watch out for in advertising. Use ideas from the article and at least one word from the Word Bank.

always • connection • family • influence • values

In your response, you should:

• Tell what teens need to watch for in advertising.

• Use details from the article in your writing.

• Use at least one word from the Word Bank.

• Use correct grammar, usage, and mechanics.

Prewrite It

Once you are sure you understand the prompt, plan what you want to say.

1. Review your notes from the class discussion. Think about the ways advertising affects teens. Begin to list your ideas on the word web.

2. Reread the article. Look for additional details to add to the web.

3. Look back at your web to see which points about advertising are the most important ones to include in your writing. Cross out the rest.

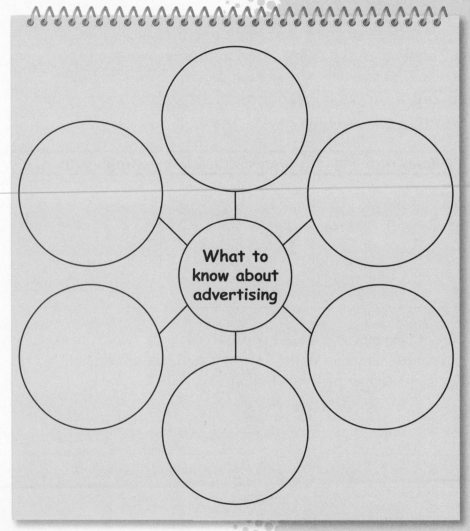

What to know about advertising

Draft It

Now use your plan to draft, or write, your advice column. The writing frame below will help you.

1. Read the note to Answer Person to begin framing your response.

2. In your response, include the most important things that teens should watch out for in advertising. Make sure your note sounds like an advice column.

Dear Answer Person,

I have a hard time deciding what to buy. Ads are everywhere!

What should I look for in advertising?

Signed, Overwhelmed

Dear Overwhelmed,

Here is what you need to know about advertising: _____

_____

_____

_____

_____

_____

Check It and Fix It

After you have written your advice, check your work. Imagine that you do not know anything about what to look for in advertising. Does this letter give information that would be helpful for you?

1. Is everything written clearly and correctly? Use the checklist on the right to see.

2. Trade your work with a classmate. Talk over ways to improve your advice. Use the ideas to revise your work.

3. For help with grammar, usage, and mechanics, go to the Handbook on pages 189–226.

If you have trouble putting your ideas into words, work with a partner. As you write, read aloud and ask your partner for feedback. Continue reading aloud to see if the work "sounds right."

✔ CHECKLIST

Evaluate your writing. A score of "5" is excellent. A score of "1" means you need to do more work. Then ask a partner to rate your work.

1. **Does the advice letter give useful ideas?**

   Me: 1 2 3 4 5
   Partner: 1 2 3 4 5

2. **Does the letter include ideas from the article?**

   Me: 1 2 3 4 5
   Partner: 1 2 3 4 5

3. **Is there at least one Word Bank word used?**

   Me: 1 2 3 4 5
   Partner: 1 2 3 4 5

4. **Are grammar, usage, and mechanics correct?**

   Me: 1 2 3 4 5
   Partner: 1 2 3 4 5

Vocabulary Workshop

Add these words to your personal word bank by practicing them.

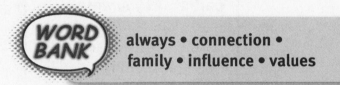

WORD BANK
always • connection • family • influence • values

Your Choice

What other new words in the article would you like to remember? List them.

_____

_____

_____

Define It

For each set of word connection boxes, choose two Word Bank words and put each word in a box. Then, in the third box, tell how those two words are connected. You will need to use one word twice.

connection	**and**	family

Connection:

	and	

Connection:

	and	

Connection:

Show You Know

To show that you understand the Word Bank words, write two sentences. In each sentence, use and highlight two words from the Word Bank. Use the example as a model.

- Your friends can influence your values.

1. _____

   _____

2. _____

   _____

Partner Up

Read your partner the sentences with the Word Bank words left out. Can your partner figure out what words go in the "blanks"? If not, you might need to rewrite to make clearer sentences.

Word Beginnings: *dis-*

- *Dis-* is a prefix that means "not" or "the opposite of." When you add *dis-* to a word, you change its meaning.

  Word without prefix: In science class we will **connect** two wires to make a circuit.

  Word with prefix: We will **disconnect** the wires after the experiment.

- Add *dis-* to the words in the chart to make new words.

Word	New Word
agree	
honest	
please	
respect	

Choose one pair of words. Use each word in a sentence.

1. _____

   _____

2. _____

   _____

ALL IN THE FAMILY

Add *-s* and *-able* to *value* to make a new word family.

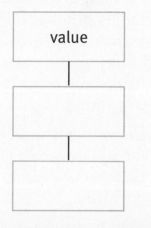

value

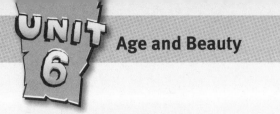

Age and Beauty

Write About It!

You have read an article about people's ideas about age and beauty. Now you will write about it. Read the writing prompt. It gives your writing assignment.

In your response, you should:

- Write a paragraph to give an idea about beauty.

- Use details from the article.

- Use at least one word from the Word Bank.

- Use correct grammar, usage, and mechanics.

Writing Prompt

After reading "Age and Beauty," what do you think beauty really is? Write a one-paragraph response explaining an unusual or unique idea of beauty. Use ideas from the article and at least one word from the Word Bank.

claim • common • culture • generation • history

Prewrite It

Once you are sure you understand the prompt, plan what you want to say.

1. Review your notes from the class discussion. Begin to fill in the organizer with your feelings about beauty and the details that helped you come to this conclusion.

2. Reread the article. Look for additional details that you can add to the organizer.

3. Your paragraph will give a description. Look at your organizer. Circle the details that are the most interesting or that will provide the best description.

> **My feelings or opinions about beauty:**
>
> **Details from the article that helped me form my opinion:**

Draft It

Now use your plan to draft, or write, your paragraph. The writing frame below will help you.

1. This paragraph will be description. Start by stating a main idea based on your own opinion about unusual or unique beauty.

2. Include details from the article as well as your own ideas about beauty.

Though it may seem unusual, something I think is beautiful is

_____

_____

The reasons I feel this way are _____

_____

_____

_____

_____

_____

_____

_____

_____

_____

Check It and Fix It

After you have written your paragraph, check over your work. Be sure that your writing gives your opinion and clearly supports it with description. Use this checklist to check your work.

1. Is everything written clearly and correctly? Use the checklist on the right to see.

2. Trade your work with a classmate. Talk over ways you both might improve your paragraphs. Use the ideas to revise your work.

3. For help with grammar, usage, and mechanics, go to the Handbook on pages 189–226.

Writing COACH

If you are having a hard time deciding what reasons to include in your paragraph, use this sentence frame: I think _____ is beautiful because _____.

✔ **CHECKLIST**

Evaluate your writing. A score of "5" is excellent. A score of "1" means you need to do more work. Then ask a partner to rate your work.

1. **Does the paragraph share a description of unusual beauty?**

   Me: 1 2 3 4 5
   Partner: 1 2 3 4 5

2. **Is information from the article included that supports the opinion?**

   Me: 1 2 3 4 5
   Partner: 1 2 3 4 5

3. **Is there at least one Word Bank word used?**

   Me: 1 2 3 4 5
   Partner: 1 2 3 4 5

4. **Are grammar, usage, and mechanics correct?**

   Me: 1 2 3 4 5
   Partner: 1 2 3 4 5

Vocabulary Workshop

Add these words to your personal word bank by practicing them.

WORD BANK claim • common • culture • generation • history

Define It

Write a word from the Word Bank on the line inside each circle. Where the circles overlap, write something that shows how the two words are the same or how they are related to each other. Write differences in the outer parts of the circles. You need to use one word twice.

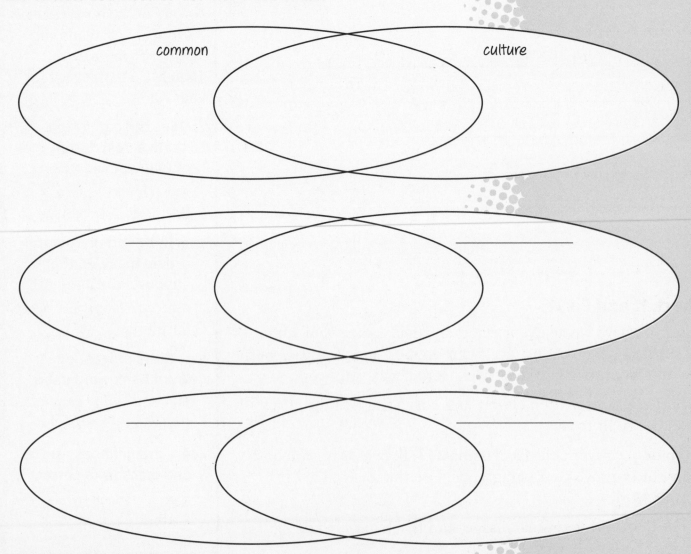

common   culture

Show You Know

Answer the questions below to show you know how each boldface Word Bank word is used.

What is something that you know you can correctly **claim**? Explain why? _____

_____

Does it help a friendship to have things in **common**? Why? _____

_____

What do you think people will learn about your **culture** in the future? _____

_____

Word Beginnings: *inter-*

- *Inter-* is a prefix. When added to the beginning of a word, *inter-* gives the meaning of something that is happening between or among similar things or groups of people.

  Word without prefix: My grandmother's **generation** does not understand how to use computers.

  Word with prefix: A reunion is an **intergenerational** family event.

- Use a dictionary to find these words with *inter-*. Write their meanings in your own words.

Interact _____

Interfere _____

Intercept _____

Intermission _____

Use two of the words in sentences that show you know the meaning of the word:

1. _____

_____

2. _____

_____

UNIT 6 WRAP UP

Writing Reflection

 How much do our communities shape us?

Look through your writing from this unit and choose the best piece. Reflect on this piece of writing by completing each sentence below.

My best piece of writing from this unit is _____

_____

I chose this piece because _____

_____

_____

While I was writing, one goal I had was _____

_____

I accomplished this goal by _____

_____

_____

This writing helped me think more about the Big Question because

_____

_____

One thing I learned while writing that can help me in the future is

_____

_____

GRAMMAR, USAGE, AND MECHANICS HANDBOOK

Nouns

A **noun** names a person, a place, or a thing.
Person: <u>Mona</u> is a <u>student</u>.
Place: My <u>school</u> is <u>Marson Middle School</u>.
Thing: That <u>article</u> is about <u>baseball</u>.

Regular Plurals

A **singular noun** names one person, place, or thing.
A **plural noun** names more than one person, place, or thing.
To form the plural of most nouns, add *–s* to the end of the noun.

Singular	Plural
one teenager	two teenager<u>s</u>
this computer	these computer<u>s</u>
that government	those government<u>s</u>
a site	many site<u>s</u>

A noncount noun, which names something you cannot count, does not have a plural form. Some common noncount nouns are *clothing, equipment, furniture, information, knowledge,* and *water.*

Exercise: Regular Plurals

Highlight and fix the five mistakes in noun plurals.

(1) There are several way to build knowledge about a subject.

(2) For example, you can look in an encyclopedia. **(3)** This helpful book has informations about many subject. **(4)** It will give you a factual explanation of each subject. **(5)** Most schools also have computer. **(6)** Student can use the Internet to search for useful facts.

NOUNS continued

Special Noun Plurals

To make some nouns plural, you need to do more than add an -s ending. Use the chart to figure out how to spell these plurals.

Singular Noun Ending	Singular	Plural
When a noun ends in *ch, s, sh, x,* or *z*, add *-es*.	a lun**ch** one dre**ss** that di**sh** this bo**x** each walt**z**	two lunch**es** many dress**es** those dish**es** these box**es** several waltz**es**
When a noun ends in a consonant + *y*, change the *y* to *i* and add *-es*.	a count**ry** one pen**ny** every ci**ty**	many count**ries** several pen**nies** ten ci**ties**
When a noun ends in *f* or *fe*, change the *f* to *v* and add *-s* or *-es*. Note: There are exceptions to this rule.	this lea**f** one kni**fe** a chie**f** one roo**f**	these lea**ves** two kni**ves** several chief**s** many roof**s**
When a noun ends in a consonant + *o*, add *-es*. Note: There are exceptions to this rule.	that he**ro** a pota**to** one pia**no** an au**to**	those hero**es** a dozen potato**es** many piano**s** several auto**s**

 **WRITER'S ALERT!** Do not use an apostrophe to form the plural of a noun.
Wrong: many belief's   **Right:** many beliefs

Exercise: Special Noun Plurals

Highlight and fix the misspelled plural in each sentence. Use the chart or a dictionary for help.

(1) Many citys have problems with graffiti. **(2)** Teenagers have tagged fences, buildings, and roofes. **(3)** In some communities, graffiti covers the sides of bus's. **(4)** The walls of subwayes are often covered with tags. **(5)** Taggers are not heros to workers who clean up their messes.

Nouns continued

Irregular Plurals

Some plural nouns do not follow the rules. Memorize common **irregular plural nouns** like the ones below.

Singular	Plural
one <u>man</u>	two <u>men</u>
a <u>woman</u>	many <u>women</u>
that <u>child</u>	those <u>children</u>
this <u>person</u>	these <u>people</u>

Exercise: Irregular Plurals

Highlight and fix the misspelled plural in each sentence.

(1) Many peoples were at the lake. **(2)** A couple of womens camped near us. **(3)** They had five childrens.

Possessive Nouns

A **possessive noun** shows ownership or relationship.
Ownership: John's coat = a coat that belongs to John
To make the possessive of a singular noun not ending in *s,* add an apostrophe and an *-s.* To make the possessive of a plural regular noun, add an apostrophe after the final *-s.*
Singular: that boy<u>'s</u> baseball **Plural:** the boys<u>'</u> baseball team

The plural of irregular nouns does not end in *-s.* Add an apostrophe and an *-s* to make them possessive.
Wrong: childrens<u>'</u> shoes   **Right:** children<u>'s</u> shoes

Exercise: Possessive Nouns

Highlight and fix the possessive noun mistake in each sentence.

(1) Marys brother Al hates elevators. **(2)** The elevator's in their building are noisy. **(3)** Many tenants complaints about the noise were ignored. **(4)** Al is scared by peoples' reactions to the noise.

Pronouns

A **pronoun** takes the place of a noun or another pronoun. The word that a pronoun refers to is its **antecedent** (an tuh SEE duhnt).

Jamal plays the guitar. He is also learning the drums.
Antecedent   Pronoun

Subject and Object Pronouns

Pronouns take different forms, depending on how they are used in sentences. A **subject pronoun** tells who or what a sentence is about. An **object pronoun** receives the action in a sentence or comes after a preposition (a word such as *for, from, in, on,* or *with*).

Subject Pronoun: She is a very fast swimmer.

Object Pronoun: The swim team gave her an award.

Object Pronoun: Swimming is fun for her.

	Singular Pronouns	**Plural Pronouns**
Used as Subjects	I you he, she, it	we you they
Used as Objects	me you him, her, it	us you them

Do not use pronouns ending in *self* as subject or object pronouns.

Wrong: She and myself are on the swim team.

Right: She and I are on the swim team.

Exercise: Subject and Object Pronouns

Underline the right pronoun form in each pair.

(1) (I, Me) love to watch Alex Rodriguez play ball.

(2) (He, Him) has hit many home runs. **(3)** Many fans consider

(he, him) to be a gift to baseball. **(4)** I agree with (they, them).

Pronouns continued

Pronouns in Compounds

Pronouns can be joined together with the word *and*. These are called **compound pronouns**.

Compound: <u>Sam and I</u> went to a movie.

Compound: The movie was exciting to <u>Sam and me.</u>

If you are not sure whether a pronoun in a compound should be in the subject form or the object form, leave out the noun. You may "hear" which form is right.

Example: My dad cooked hamburgers for ~~my brother and~~ (I, <u>me</u>).

Exercise: Pronouns in Compounds

Highlight and fix the pronoun mistake in each sentence.

(1) Juan and me did a project for science class. **(2)** Him and I decided to study water pollution. **(3)** Taking samples from the lake was easy for him and I. **(4)** Analyzing them was harder, but he and me did it. **(5)** The teacher gave Juan and I an A.

Possessive Pronouns

Possessive pronouns show who owns something. They can be used to describe nouns or in place of possessive nouns.

	Singular	Plural
Describer	<u>my</u> book <u>your</u> book <u>his</u>, <u>her</u>, <u>its</u> book	<u>our</u> books <u>your</u> books <u>their</u> books
Noun Substitute	<u>Mine</u> has my name in it. Did you forget <u>yours</u>? <u>His</u> and <u>hers</u> are missing.	<u>Ours</u> are here. <u>Yours</u> are there. <u>Theirs</u> are missing.

Exercise: Possessive Pronouns

Highlight and fix the pronoun mistake in each sentence.

(1) That book is mines. **(2)** It is not your's. **(3)** The other book is their. **(4)** Hers book is at home.

Pronouns continued

Demonstrative Pronouns

The words *this*, *that*, *these*, and *those* are **demonstrative** (di MAHN struh tiv) **pronouns**. They point to a specific person, place, or thing. *This* and *these* point to things near the speaker. *That* and *those* point to things farther away. *This* and *that* are singular. *These* and *those* are plural.

Never use *them* as a demonstrative pronoun.
Wrong: Bring me <u>them</u> books.
Right: Bring me <u>those</u> books.

Exercise: Demonstrative Pronouns

<u>Underline</u> the right pronoun to use in each pair.

(1) (This, That) bus stop is far away. **(2)** I would rather wait at (this, that) bus stop, here. **(3)** Have you ever ridden on one of (them, those) double-decker buses?

Indefinite Pronouns

Indefinite pronouns refer to people, places, or things that are not specifically identified. Some indefinite pronouns are always singular. Others are always plural.

Singular	anybody everybody no one	anyone everyone nothing	anything everything somebody	each neither someone	either nobody something
Plural	both	few	many	several	

Exercise: Indefinite Pronouns

Highlight the indefinite pronoun in each sentence. Write *S* above the pronoun if it is singular or *P* if it is plural.

(1) Everyone is excited. **(2)** Each of us has a ticket to the museum. **(3)** Many of us have never before been to a science museum. **(4)** No one is sure what to expect. **(5)** Anyone who wants can visit the museum Web site before we go.

Pronouns continued

Pronoun-Antecedent Agreement

A pronoun and its antecedent—the word the pronoun stands for—must **agree,** or match. To match in number, both a pronoun and its antecedent must be singular or plural.

Wrong: <u>Nobody</u> raised <u>their</u> hand.
singular   plural

Right: <u>Nobody</u> raised <u>his or her</u> hand.
singular   singular

Use the chart to figure out how to make pronouns and their antecedents agree.

	Singular	Plural
First person	<u>I</u> have <u>my</u> pen.	<u>We</u> have <u>our</u> pens.
Second person	<u>You</u> have <u>your</u> pen.	<u>You</u> have <u>your</u> pens.
Third person	<u>He</u> has <u>his</u> pen.	<u>They</u> have <u>their</u> pens.

WRITER'S ALERT!

To avoid using the phrase *his or her,* make both the antecedent and the pronoun plural.
Singular: <u>Everybody</u> brought <u>his or her</u> ticket.
Plural: <u>All the students</u> brought <u>their</u> tickets.

Exercise: Pronoun-Antecedent Agreement

Highlight and fix the pronoun mistake in each sentence.

1. Everybody brought their skateboard to the park.

2. Manny did the jump it has been practicing.

3. Each skater worked to master their skills.

4. No one wanted to go back to their classroom.

Pronouns continued

Relative Pronouns

A **relative pronoun** is used to introduce a clause (a group of words containing a verb and its subject). The relative pronoun *relates* the clause to the rest of the sentence.

Relative Clause: Marisa is the student <u>who won the award</u>.

relative
pronoun

Relative Pronouns
who, whom, whose, whoever, whomever, which, what, that

Use relative pronouns to combine two or three short, choppy sentences into one smooth sentence.
Choppy: The music is good. The music is on the radio.
Better: The music <u>that is on the radio</u> is good.

Exercise: Relative Pronouns

Use the relative pronoun in parentheses to combine each pair of sentences into one sentence.

1. (that) Beau was the ugliest dog. He was in the shelter.

_____.

2. (who) People went to the shelter. They did not notice him.

_____.

3. (who) I was the only one. I wanted to adopt Beau.

_____.

4. (that) My family is glad. We adopted him.

_____.

Verbs

A **verb** expresses action or links important parts of a sentence together. Every sentence has at least one verb. The verb is the main word or group of words in the **predicate** (PRE duh kuht), which is the part of the sentence that tells about the subject.

Example: <u>Bob</u> <u>is</u> my brother.

The sentence is about Bob, so *Bob* is the subject. The verb *is* links *Bob* to *my brother*, which tells who Bob is. That makes *is* the verb in the predicate.

Example: <u>Bob</u> <u>writes</u> wonderful songs.

The sentence is about Bob, so *Bob* is the subject. The verb *writes* tells what Bob does, so *writes* is the verb in the predicate.

Action Verbs and Linking Verbs

Many **action verbs** name an action you can see—for example, *run, jump, smile*. Other action verbs name an action you cannot see—for example, *think, wonder, hope*. An action verb may stand alone with a subject to state a complete thought, or it may have an **object**—a person, place, or thing that receives or shows the result of the action.

Subject and Action Verb: <u>Darnella</u> <u>dances</u>.
                                        subject   verb

Subject, Action Verb, and Object: <u>Carmelita</u> <u>plays</u> <u>piano</u>.
                                                subject   verb   object

Linking verbs do not show action. Instead, they connect subjects with **complements**. Complements help complete the thought that subjects and their linking verbs begin to express. The most common linking verbs are forms of *to be: am, is, are, was, were, being, been*.

Thought Seems Incomplete: <u>Terrell</u> <u>is</u>.

Thought Is Complete: <u>Terrell</u> <u>is</u> a <u>firefighter</u>.

Exercise: Action Verbs and Linking Verbs

Highlight each action verb. <u>Underline</u> each linking verb.

(1) Larissa is a hero. (2) She sailed down the river with some kids from camp. (3) Their raft hit a big rock. (4) Shawn fell off the raft.

(5) Larissa jumped into the water. (6) She swam to Shawn.

(7) He was hurt. (8) Larissa helped Shawn. (9) We are grateful.

(10) Shawn is now OK.

Verbs continued

Present Tense Verbs

The **tense** of a verb tells the time of an action or a state of being. It may tell when an action happened, happens, or will happen—in the past, the present, or the future. Use the **present tense** to something that happens or exists in the present, happens regularly, or is always true.

Happens Regularly: I <u>enjoy</u> the sunset nearly every day.

Always True: The sun <u>sets</u> in the west.

Use the chart below to form the present tense of **regular verbs** (verbs that follow regular rules). Notice that the form of a present tense verb depends on the subject that goes with it. If the subject is *he, she,* or *it,* the verb ends in *-s.* If the subject is *I, you, we,* or *they,* the verb does not end in *-s.*

Singular	Plural
I <u>like</u> you <u>like</u> he, she, it <u>likes</u>	we <u>like</u> you <u>like</u> they <u>like</u>

If a subject is a noun and you are not sure which verb form to use, change the noun into the pronoun that could substitute for it. Then use the chart.

Noun Subject: <u>Victor</u> (like, likes) rap.

Pronoun Subject: *Victor = he.* <u>Victor</u> (like, <u>likes</u>) rap.

Exercise: Present Tense Verbs

<u>Underline</u> the right verb form in parentheses. Use the chart if you need to.

(1) Will (bike, bikes) almost every day. (2) Will and Eric (shiver, shivers) in the winter. (3) Even so, if the roads are clear of snow, the boys (take, takes) their bikes to school. (4) That way, Will and Eric (get, gets) enough exercise. (5) Will (want, wants) to become a professional cyclist some day.

Verbs continued

Tricky Present Tense Verbs

Some verbs do not form the present tense in the regular way, by adding -s. The only way to learn tricky verbs like *have, do,* and *be* is to memorize them. Study the chart.

	Have	Do	Be
Singular	I <u>have</u> (<u>haven't</u>) you <u>have</u> (<u>haven't</u>) he, she, it <u>has</u> (<u>hasn't</u>)	I <u>do</u> (<u>don't</u>) you <u>do</u> (<u>don't</u>) he, she, it <u>does</u> (<u>doesn't</u>)	I am (<u>I'm</u> not) you are (<u>aren't</u>) he, she, it <u>is</u>, (<u>isn't</u>)
Plural	we <u>have</u> (<u>haven't</u>) you <u>have</u> (<u>haven't</u>) they <u>have</u> (<u>haven't</u>)	we <u>do</u> (<u>don't</u>) you <u>do</u> (<u>don't</u>) they <u>do</u> (<u>don't</u>)	we <u>are</u> (<u>aren't</u>) you <u>are</u> (<u>aren't</u>) they <u>are</u> (<u>aren't</u>)

These tricky verbs can stand alone as **main verbs,** or they can be helping verbs. A **helping verb** helps a main verb express action or give a statement.

Main Verb: Sinclair <u>has</u> a cell phone.
Helping Verb + Main Verb: Sinclair <u>has</u> <u>called</u> me on her phone.

> Avoid using *ain't.*
> **Wrong:** I <u>ain't</u> tired.
> **Right:** I <u>am</u> <u>not</u> tired. OR <u>I'm</u> <u>not</u> tired.
> **Wrong:** He <u>ain't</u> here.
> **Right:** He <u>is</u> <u>not</u> here. OR He <u>isn't</u> here.

Exercise: Tricky Present Tense Verbs

Highlight and fix the six verb mistakes in the paragraph.

(1) I ain't walking down that hallway. (2) I do not want to open that big gray door at the end. (3) Don't you hear something? (4) Something do not feel right. (5) I have been nervous all day. (6) You ain't helping. (7) I am ready to go home. (8) It sure do feel like three o'clock by now. (9) This ain't fun. (10) Has you got bus fare?

Verbs continued

Agreement with Compound Subjects

A **compound subject** is two or more subjects joined by the word *and* or *or*. When the subjects are joined by *and,* the compound subject is usually plural. To match, or agree with this compound subject, the verb must be in the plural form. When the subjects are joined by *or,* the verb must agree with the subject closer to it, whether singular or plural.

Compound with *And:* <u>Benoit and I</u> (is, <u>are</u>) friends.
Compound with *Or:* Benoit or <u>I</u> (<u>am</u>, is, are) happy to help.
Compound with *Or:* I or <u>Benoit</u> (am, <u>is</u>, are) happy to help.

Exercise: Agreement with Compound Subjects

Highlight and fix the three verb mistakes.

(1) Laila and Hilary are shooting baskets. **(2)** Hilary and I is best friends. **(3)** Laila or Hilary have been chosen team captain.

(4) The coach or her assistant know which girl has been chosen.

(5) You and I have to wait for the announcement.

Agreement in Questions

In most questions, all or part of the verb comes before the subject. The verb at the beginning of a question must agree with the subject.

Statement: <u>Thomasina</u> <u>is</u> <u>going</u> to the party.
              subject   verb

Question: <u>Is</u> <u>Thomasina</u> <u>going</u> to the party?
         verb   subject   verb

Exercise: Agreement in Questions

For each sentence, <u>underline</u> the right verb in parentheses.

(1) (Are, Is) you familiar with the music of Joe Syne?

(2) What (do, does) you like to listen to? **(3)** (Have, Has) any famous musicians come to your city recently? **(4)** Where (do, does) a live band play around here? **(5)** (Are, Is) Matt and Joe in a band?

Verbs continued

Past and Perfect Tenses

Use the **past tense** of a verb to express action that happened in the past or a situation that existed at a certain time in the past. To form the past tense of a regular verb, add an *-ed* ending.

Past: Yesterday, Lucie <u>called</u> me on her new phone.

Use the **present perfect tense** to express action that began in the past and is still happening or that happened at an indefinite time in the past. To form the present perfect, use the helping verb *has* or *have*.

Present Perfect: People <u>have</u> <u>used</u> cell phones since the 1970s.

Use the **past perfect tense** to express an action that was completed before another action in the past. To form the past perfect, use the helping verb *had*.

Past Perfect: I <u>had</u> already <u>left</u> the house when Lucie called.

	Present Perfect *have* or *has* + verb + *-ed*	Past Perfect *had* + verb +*-ed*
Singular	I <u>have</u> <u>walked</u> you <u>have</u> <u>walked</u> he, she, it <u>has</u> <u>walked</u>	I <u>had</u> <u>walked</u> you <u>had</u> <u>walked</u> he, she, it <u>had</u> <u>walked</u>
Plural	we <u>have</u> <u>walked</u> you <u>have</u> <u>walked</u> they <u>have</u> <u>walked</u>	we <u>had</u> <u>walked</u> you <u>had</u> <u>walked</u> they <u>had</u> <u>walked</u>

The helping verb must agree with the subject.
Wrong: <u>Haven't</u> <u>he</u> listened to the news?
Right: <u>Hasn't</u> <u>he</u> listened to the news?

Exercise: Past and Perfect Tenses

Highlight and fix the verb mistake in each sentence.

(1) Leon have cared about animals all his life. (2) By the time he was six, he had decide to become a veterinarian. (3) For the past three years, he has volunteer at the animal shelter. (4) Leon explains to our class yesterday that one cat can have three litters a year.

(5) He warn us that many kittens end up in shelters.

Verbs continued

Irregular Verbs 1: Past and Perfect of *To Be*

Irregular verbs do not take an -*ed* ending to form the past and perfect tenses. The most irregular verb in English is *to be*.

	Past Tense	Present Perfect Tense
Singular	I <u>was</u> (<u>wasn't</u>) you <u>were</u> (<u>weren't</u>) he, she, it <u>was</u> (<u>wasn't</u>)	I <u>have</u> (<u>haven't</u>) <u>been</u> you <u>have</u> (<u>haven't</u>) <u>been</u> he, she, it <u>has</u> (<u>hasn't</u>) <u>been</u>
Plural	we <u>were</u> (<u>weren't</u>) you <u>were</u> (<u>weren't</u>) they <u>were</u> (<u>weren't</u>)	we <u>have</u> (<u>haven't</u>) <u>been</u> you <u>have</u> (<u>haven't</u>) <u>been</u> they <u>have</u> (<u>haven't</u>) been

	Past Perfect Tense
Singular	I <u>had</u> (<u>hadn't</u>) <u>been</u> you <u>had</u> (<u>hadn't</u>) <u>been</u> he, she, it <u>had</u> (<u>hadn't</u>) <u>been</u>
Plural	we <u>had</u> (<u>hadn't</u>) <u>been</u> you <u>had</u> (<u>hadn't</u>) <u>been</u> they <u>had</u> (<u>hadn't</u>) <u>been</u>

Exercise: Irregular Verbs 1: Past and Perfect of *To Be*

Highlight and fix the verb mistake in each sentence.

(1) Andy Warhol were a famous artist. **(2)** Warhol and his friends was the inventors of pop art. **(3)** Pop artists was interested in popular culture. **(4)** Their art were about movie stars, comic strips, and even soup cans. **(5)** Their paintings been popular for years.

Irregular Verbs 2: Past and Perfect That Stay the Same

Some irregular verbs keep the same form for every tense. The most common are *cost, cut, hit, let, put, read, set,* and *shut.*
Present: I <u>read</u> every day.
Past: Yesterday, I <u>read</u> the sports pages.
Present Perfect: I <u>have</u> <u>read</u> ten books this year.
Past Perfect: My mom gave me a book, but I <u>had</u> already <u>read</u> it.

Verbs continued

Irregular Verbs 3: Past and Perfect That Change Vowels

Some irregular verbs change only a vowel to go from present tense to past or perfect. Others add -*n* or -*en* to form the perfect tenses.

Present Tense	Past Tense	Perfect Tenses (has, have, had)
become	became	become
begin	began	begun
break	broke	broken
come	came	come
drink	drank	drunk
drive	drove	driven
forget	forgot	forgotten
give	gave	given
grow	grew	grown
know	knew	known
ride	rode	ridden
ring	rang	rung
rise	rose	risen
run	ran	run
see	saw	seen
sing	sang	sung
sit	sat	sat
speak	spoke	spoken
swim	swam	swum
write	wrote	written

Exercise: Irregular Verbs 3: Past and Perfect That Change Vowels

Highlight and fix the verb mistake in each sentence.

(1) When choir camp begun, I was nervous. (2) I had came all the way from Texas to New York. (3) Then I run into two kids I knew. (4) They had sang in my choral group. (5) I seen them the first day, so I relaxed.

Verbs continued

Irregular Verbs 4: Past and Perfect That Change Completely

Some verbs change their form completely to form the past or perfect tenses. Many of them (like *bring* and *buy*) have the same form for past and perfect tenses. A few (like *do* and *fly*) have different forms for past and perfect tenses.

Present Tense	Past Tense	Perfect Tenses (has, have, had)
bring	brought	brought
buy	bought	bought
catch	caught	caught
do	did	done
fight	fought	fought
find	found	found
fly	flew	flown
go	went	gone
sell	sold	sold
take	took	taken
teach	taught	taught
think	thought	thought

Exercise: Irregular Verbs 4: Past and Perfect That Change Completely

Highlight and fix the verb mistake in each sentence.

(1) At dusk, we watched as an owl flyed down to catch a mouse. (2) I thought it would succeed, but the owl missed and flown into a tree. (3) My father finded it lying on the ground. (4) He catched it carefully. (5) He brang it over to show us. (6) After we had took it to a bird center, we waited. (7) Finally, a trainer called to say the owl had flew again at last. (8) She had teached it to catch mice again. (9) She thunk it was ready to go back to the wild. (10) She invited us to watch her set it free, so we boughten a camera.

Verbs continued

Verbs as Describers

Certain verb forms can act as describers. These **verbals** describe nouns or pronouns. Verbals can end in *-ing, -ed,* or, when the verb is irregular, the perfect form. Be sure to use the right ending or form.

Verbal: A <u>freezing</u> rain fell.

Verbal: Chantel wore <u>faded</u> jeans.

Verbal: Her favorite jeans have a <u>broken</u> zipper.

Exercise: Verbs as Describers

Highlight and fix the three mistakes in verbals.

(1) I like cooking shows. **(2)** The Asian chef made fry rice.

(3) She seasoned it with home-growed herbs. **(4)** For dessert,

she served a freshly bake cake.

Future Tense

The **future tense** expresses action that will happen in the future.
To form the future tense, use the helping verb *will* and a main verb.
Present: I <u>walk</u> to school every day.
Future: I <u>will</u> <u>walk</u> to soccer practice after school today.

Exercise: Future Tense

Change each <u>underlined</u> verb to future tense.

(1) Next week, we <u>go</u> _____ to Michigan. **(2)** We <u>camped</u>

_____ in a national park. **(3)** We <u>hike</u> _____ every day.

(4) We <u>swam</u> _____ in Lake Ritchie. **(5)** We <u>cooked</u>

_____ dinner over a campfire.

Verbs continued

Progressive Tenses

The **progressive tense** expresses action in progress, or still happening. To form the present and past progressive, use a form of *to be* and a main verb with an *-ing* ending. To form the future progressive, add the future-tense helping word *will*.

Present Progressive: I <u>am</u> <u>biking</u>.
Past Progressive: I <u>was</u> <u>biking</u>.
Future Progressive: I <u>will be</u> <u>biking</u>.

Exercise: Progressive Tenses

Write a sentence to answer each question below. Make sure your answers are in the correct tenses.

1. What were you doing just before you started reading this?

_____

2. What will you be doing over the summer?

_____

3. What are you doing right now?

_____

Modals

Modals are helping verbs. They include *can, could, will, would, must, should, may, might,* and *ought to.* A main verb paired with a modal never takes an ending such as *-ed* or *-s*. It does not change form.

Wrong: I <u>should</u> **called** him.   **Right:** I <u>should</u> **call** him.
Wrong: She <u>can</u> **sings**.   **Right:** She <u>can</u> **sing**.

Exercise: Modals

Highlight and fix the four verb mistakes.

(1) You should comes to Ari's party. (2) I might go. (3) You will loved his video games. (4) Last year, we played games for hours.

(5) I may stopped at the mall first. (6) I could bought a gift for him.

Adjectives

Adjectives describe nouns and pronouns. Adjectives answer these questions: *Which one? What kind? How many? How much?*

Which One: The blue coat is mine.

What Kind: It is a wool coat.

How Many: I own two coats.

How Much: That is enough coats for anyone.

Articles

The most often used adjectives are the **articles**: *a, an,* and *the. The* is called a **definite article**, because it is used to refer to a particular person, place, or thing. *A* and *an* are called **indefinite articles**, because they do not refer to a particular person, place, or thing.

Definite Article: Buy your ticket from the man in the booth.

Indefinite Article: A ticket costs $10.

Use *a* with words that begin with a consonant sound. Use *an* with words that begin with a vowel sound. (It is the *sound* that matters, not the spelling.)

A: a car, a song, a unit (*u* with the consonant *y* sound)
An: an ant, an olive, an umbrella (*u* with the vowel *u* sound)

Use *a* or *an* if the noun can be counted.
Example: I spilled a cup of coffee. (You can count a cup.)
Use *the* if the noun cannot be counted.
Example: I spilled the coffee. (You cannot count coffee that is not in a cup.)

Exercise: Articles

Highlight and fix the five mistakes involving articles.

(1) My family went on an photo safari to Africa. **(2)** It was the trip of a lifetime. **(3)** I saw a elephant with a baby. **(4)** My sister saw an lion. **(5)** The guide said it was an oldest lion in the park. **(6)** The animals walk freely around the park. **(7)** A freedom allows them to live naturally.

Adjectives continued

Adjectives That Compare

Adjectives can be used to make comparisons. Use the **comparative** (kuhm PER uh tiv) **adjective** form to compare two people, places, or things. To form the comparative of one-syllable adjectives and many two-syllable adjectives, add *-er*. To form the comparative of adjectives of three or more syllables, add the word *more* or *less* in front of the adjective.

One-Syllable Adjective: Sara is <u>younger</u> than I am.
Three-Syllable Adjective: I am <u>more</u> <u>athletic</u> than she is.

Use the **superlative** (soo PUHR luh tiv) **adjective** form to compare three or more people, places, or things. To form the superlative of one-syllable adjectives and many two-syllable adjectives, add *-est*. To form the superlative of adjectives of three or more syllables, add the word *most* or *least* in front of the adjective.

One-Syllable Adjective: Caryn is the <u>oldest</u> girl in our family.
Three-Syllable Adjective: She is our <u>most</u> <u>talented</u> musician.

 Some adjectives can take a comparative or superlative ending OR *more* or *most*. When in doubt, check a dictionary.

Exercise: Adjectives That Compare

Fill in each blank with the right form of the adjective in parentheses.

1. Enrique is _____ than his brother Javier. **(old)**

2. However, he is _____ than his sister Francie. **(young)**

3. Francie is the _____ child in the family. **(old)**

4. She is the _____ actress in the senior class. **(talented)**

5. She starred in the class play, the _____ ever. **(popular)**

Adjectives continued

Irregular Adjectives

Not all adjectives form comparisons in regular ways. The chart shows how to form common irregular adjectives.

Adjective	Comparative	Superlative
good, well	better	best
bad	worse	worst
many, much	more	most
little	less	least

Exercise: Irregular Adjectives

Fill in each blank with the right form of the adjective in parentheses.

1. Tony is a _____ skateboarder than his brother. **(good)**

2. Tony has won _____ contests than I have. **(many)**

3. He has broken the _____ bones of all! **(many)**

4. Injuries are the _____ part of the sport. **(bad)**

Double Comparisons

Never use *more* or *most* with an adjective that ends with *-er* or *-est*. This mistake in grammar is called a **double comparison.**
Wrong: My hometown is the <u>most</u> <u>bestest</u> place on earth.
Right: My hometown is the <u>best</u> place on earth.

Wrong: It is <u>more</u> <u>warmer</u> here than in Miami.
Right: It is <u>warmer</u> here than in Miami.

Exercise: Double Comparisons

Highlight and fix the three adjective mistakes.

　　(1) The most longest day of the year is the summer solstice.

(2) It is light outside more longer in June than in August. **(3)** In the southern hemisphere, the shortest day is in June. **(4)** There, it is more colder in June than in January.

Adverbs

Adverbs describe verbs, adjectives, and other adverbs. Adverbs answer these questions: *How? When? Where? How much? How often?*

How: Jim spoke <u>quietly</u>.

When: He is <u>never</u> loud.

Where: He arrived <u>here</u> at five o'clock.

How much? or **How often?:** He <u>usually</u> gets here by four o'clock.

The *-ly* Adverb Ending

Many adverbs are formed by adding *-ly* to the end of an adjective.

Example: quiet + ly = quietly

Not all adverbs end in *-ly*, however, and not every word that ends in *-ly* is an adverb. For example, the word *friendly* ends in *-ly*, but it is an adjective, not an adverb.

The word *real* is an adjective. The word *really* is an adverb. Use *really* when you are describing an adjective.
Wrong: Sherelle is <u>real</u> happy.
Right: Sherelle is <u>really</u> happy.

Exercise: The *-ly* Adverb Ending

Add *-ly* to each adjective in parentheses to form an adverb.

1. Sherelle can sing _____. **(beautiful)**

2. After she sings, the audience claps _____. **(loud)**

3. She _____ takes a bow. **(quick)**

4. The audience makes her grin _____. **(happy)**

5. She _____ leaves the stage. **(graceful)**

Adverbs continued

Good and *Well*

Use the adjective *good* to describe people, places, and things.

Example: That is a good song.

Use *well* as an adverb to describe action verbs and adjectives.
Use *well* as an adjective to describe someone's health.

Example: The band played well.

Example: *Jen* felt well after a good night's rest.

Exercise: *Good* and *Well*

Highlight and fix the two mistakes in the use of *good* and *well*.

(1) Abhi did good in the marathon. **(2)** He got off to a good start. **(3)** He did not feel good the next day, though.

Double Negatives

Do not form a **double negative** by using two negative words in the same clause. The adverb *not* is negative. So are contractions that contain the word *not* (*can't, don't, haven't, isn't, wasn't,* and so on). To fix a double negative, change one of the negatives into a positive, or drop one of the negative words.

Wrong: I don't have no money.

Right: I don't have any money. OR I have no money.

Negatives	Positives
never	ever
nobody, no one	somebody, someone
none	some
nothing	something, anything
nowhere	somewhere
hardly, barely	_____

Exercise: Double Negatives

Highlight and fix the double negative in each sentence.

(1) Ray could not hardly breathe. **(2)** He hadn't never felt so sick.

(3) He wouldn't ask nobody to taste that medicine.

Prepositions

A **preposition** (pre puh ZI shuhn) shows the relationship between a noun or pronoun and another word in a sentence.

Example: The stars shone <u>above</u> us.

Example: We sat <u>on</u> a bench <u>beside</u> the lake.

Prepositions					
about	among	beneath	for	on	under
above	around	beside	from	onto	underneath
across	at	between	in	over	until
after	before	beyond	into	through	with
against	behind	by	near	to	within
along	below	during	of	toward	without

Prepositional Phrases

A **prepositional phrase** is a group of words that go together and that begin with a preposition and end with a noun or pronoun. The noun or pronoun at the end of the phrase is called the **object of the preposition.**

Prepositional Phrase: The moon rose <u>over the calm lake</u>.

preposition   object

Exercise: Prepositional Phrases

<u>Underline</u> the prepositional phrase in each sentence below.

(1) My friend Maya and I volunteer at the local hospital.

(2) The hospital has a big playroom for young kids. **(3)** We babysit them and play with them. **(4)** Yesterday, one of the kids disappeared.

(5) I found him hiding under a chair!

Conjunctions

Conjunctions (kuhn JUHNG shuhns) connect, or join, words or groups of words. There are three kinds of conjunctions:

1. coordinating

2. correlative

3. subordinating

Coordinating Conjunctions

Coordinating (koh AWR duh nay ting) **conjunctions** connect similar words or groups of words. They can link parts of sentences or whole sentences. The coordinating conjunctions are as follows:

Coordinating Conjunctions
and, but, for, nor, or, so, yet

Sentence Parts: Kim and her mom went on a trip.

Sentences: They went to Ohio, and they saw the Columbus Zoo.

Exercise: Coordinating Conjunctions

Highlight the coordinating conjunction in each sentence.

1. Luis and I went to Pittsburgh.

2. We wanted to see a Steelers game, but the football season was over.

3. We went to a Pirates game, and we had a lot of fun.

4. Do you like baseball or football?

5. I like them both, for both are interesting sports.

6. I play football, yet I also like baseball.

7. I want to play well, so I practice often.

8. I was not chosen to be quarterback, nor did I want to be.

Conjunctions continued

Subordinating Conjunctions

A **subordinating** (suh BAWR duh nay ting) **conjunction** introduces and connects a subordinate clause to a main clause.

Subordinating Conjunctions			
after	because	since	until
although	before	so that	when
as	even though	than	where
as if	if	though	whereas
as though	in order that	unless	while

Example: While we were in Chicago, we visited museums.
            subordinate clause   main clause

Exercise: Subordinating Conjunctions

Highlight the subordinating conjunction in each sentence and underline the subordinate clause.

(1) I take guitar lessons because I want to be a great guitarist.

(2) Since I was ten years old, I have wanted to play in a band. **(3)** If my older brother would let me, I would play in his band.

Correlative Conjunctions

Correlative (kuh RE luh tiv) **conjunctions** work in pairs.

both . . . and	either . . . or
not only . . . but also	neither . . . nor

Example: Both Lia and Raj are in the chess club.
Example: Neither Lia nor Raj likes to lose.

Exercise: Correlative Conjunctions

Highlight the correlative conjunctions in each sentence.

(1) Both Rena and her sister are talented. **(2)** Rena not only dances but also sings. **(3)** Neither my sister nor I sing or dance.

Sentences

A **complete sentence** is a group of words that has a subject and a predicate and that expresses a complete thought. The **subject** tells who or what the sentence is about. The predicate tells what the subject is or does.

Complete Sentence: <u>Josephina</u> <u>overslept this morning</u>.

                  subject   predicate

There are four types of sentences.

1. A **declarative** (di KLER uh tiv) sentence makes a statement.

- <u>Josephina</u> <u>missed</u> her bus.

2. An **imperative** (im PER uh tiv) sentence gives an order.

- <u>Set</u> the alarm. (The "understood" subject is <u>you</u>.)

3. An **exclamatory** (iks KLA muh tawr ee) sentence shows emotion.

- What a nightmare <u>she</u> <u>had</u>!

4. An **interrogative** (in tuh RAH guh tiv) sentence asks a question.

- What time <u>did</u> <u>she</u> <u>go</u> to bed last night?

Clauses

A **clause** is a group of words that contains a verb and its subject. A **main clause** can stand alone as a sentence. A **subordinate clause** begins with a subordinating conjunction. A subordinate clause cannot stand alone. It must be joined to a main clause.

Main clause: <u>Lenny</u> <u>is</u> afraid to speak in public.

Subordinate clause: because <u>he</u> <u>is</u> very shy

Sentence: Lenny is afraid to speak in public because he is very shy.

Exercise: Clauses

<u>Underline</u> the subordinate clause in each sentence below.

(1) Lara gave her oral report when I gave mine. **(2)** She reported on the race horse Seabiscuit because she loves horses. **(3)** As she talked, I tried to concentrate. **(4)** It was my turn after Lara spoke.

Sentences continued

Run-on Sentences

A **run-on sentence** is a common kind of mistake in writing. A run-on happens when two or more sentences are written as one sentence. There are three kinds of run-on sentences:

1. Main clauses are separated only by a comma.

- Roy walked home, it was autumn.

2. Main clauses are not separated by any punctuation.

- The sky was blue the leaves were red and gold.

3. Main clauses are separated by a coordinating conjunction, but the comma before the conjunction is missing.

- He felt like running but he did not want to make any noise.

Here are two ways to fix a run-on sentence.

Fix 1: Separate the main clauses, or sentences, with a period.

- Roy walked home. It was autumn.

Fix 2: Add a comma and a coordinating conjunction (if the sentences are not already separated by a coordinating conjunction).

- The sky was blue, and the leaves were red and gold.
- He felt like running, but he did not want to make any noise.

Exercise: Run-on Sentences

Find and fix the four run-on sentences below. There is more than one right way to fix each sentence.

(1) One teen was at a fast-food place, he had an idea.

(2) He saw some people using sign language to order but they needed an interpreter. (3) He invented a computer, it could translate sign language. (4) This invention helps deaf people live more independently, it saves time. (5) Inventing new things is fun, so why don't you try it?

Sentences continued

Fragments

A **sentence fragment** is an incomplete sentence that is capitalized and punctuated as if it were complete. Common reasons for fragments are as follows:

1. The sentence is missing a subject.

Fragment: <u>Went</u> to a storytelling festival.
Complete: <u>Al and Beatrice</u> <u>went</u> to a storytelling festival.

2. The sentence is missing a verb.

Fragment: <u>Al and Beatrice</u> to a storytelling festival.
Complete: <u>Al and Beatrice</u> <u>went</u> to a storytelling festival.

3. The subordinate clause is not connected to a main clause.

Fragment: When they got to the festival.
Complete: When they got to the festival, they saw some friends.

Exercise: Fragments

Follow the directions in parentheses to fix each fragment.

1. (Add a subject.) _____ love to listen to music.

2. (Add a verb.) I _____ to the radio all the time.

3. (Add a main clause.) _____
since it plays my favorite music.

4. (Add a verb.) What kind of music _____ your favorite?

5. (Add a main clause.) Whatever music you prefer. _____
_____

Capitalization

Capitalize proper nouns and proper adjectives. A **proper noun** names a specific person, place, or thing. A **common noun** does not. A **proper adjective** is an adjective formed from a proper noun.

Common	Proper
man	Damion
school	Dawes Middle School

Capitalize the following.

1. The proper name or title of a person:
- Sue, R. G., Dad, Ms. Smith, Detective Jones, President Adams

2. The proper name of a place:
- Chicago, Utah, France, Main Street, the Sears Tower

3. A proper adjective:
- American, British, Chinese

4. The first word of a sentence:
- The night was dark.

5. A letter's salutation and the first word of the closing:
- Dear Madam or Sir: • Sincerely yours,

6. The first word, last word, and all main words in the title of a work:
- *The Sound of Music*

Exercise: Capitalization
Highlight and fix the capitalization mistakes in each sentence.

(1) Dear uncle Len,

(2) We had the best time on vacation in new York! (3) We went to the top of the empire state building. (4) then we went to see a play. (5) It was called *a Raisin in the sun*. (6) Afterward, we went out for mexican food.

Punctuation

Punctuation helps readers understand how sentences should be read. **Punctuation marks** include commas, apostrophes, quotation marks, and end marks (periods, question marks, exclamation points).

A **comma** signals a pause or separates parts of a sentence:
• When the phone rang, he answered.
• Cleveland, Ohio, is her home.

An **apostrophe** can show possession, show where letters are missing in a contraction, or show that a letter or number is plural.
• Sara's ears almost froze when she didn't wear her hat.
• Several members of the class got straight A's.

Quotation marks set off someone's exact words. They are also used to set off titles of articles, short stories, and episodes of TV shows.
• "What did you say?" Homer asked.
• My favorite show is "Pole to Pole."

End Marks
An **end mark** goes at the end of a sentence.
A **period** ends a complete sentence that makes a statement:
• Roz went to school early today.
A **question mark** ends a direct question:
• Why did she go early?
An **exclamation point** ends a sentence that shows strong emotion:
• Do not spill that juice!

 Put periods and commas inside closing quotation marks. "I am glad," Maria said, " to meet you at last."

Exercise: End Marks
Add the correct end mark to each sentence.

(1) Nate and I are on a softball team (2) He hit a long line drive

(3) I yelled, "Run, run" (4) He just stood there (5) Later I asked,

"Why didn't you run" (6) He said, "I don't know"

Punctuation continued

Commas

Use commas in the following situations:

1. To separate three or more items in a series:

- They walked past shops, houses, and parks.

2. To set off names and titles used in direct address:

- Have you seen my CD, Tim?

3. To set off dates and addresses:

- On July 25, 1999, my sister was born in St. George, Utah.

4. After an introductory word, phrase, or clause:

- Finally, the day ended. At last, we relaxed. If you want, sleep.

5. To set off explainers:

- LaTise, our class president, does a good job.
- Soccer, which is my favorite sport, involves a lot of running.

6. To separate clauses joined by a coordinating conjunction:

- Ron did his homework, but Ken did not do his.

Do not use a comma to separate the parts of a compound predicate:

Wrong: Ron did his math, but not his writing.

Right: Ron did his math but not his writing.

Exercise: Commas

Add the missing comma or commas to each sentence.

(1) Lynn have you ever been to a poetry slam? **(2)** People perform poems and others judge how well they did. **(3)** Fortunately there are poetry slams for kids. **(4)** I went to my first slam on June 10 2008 in my hometown. **(5)** Russ my friend from down the street went with me. **(6)** Russ Nikki and I all enjoy slams. **(7)** We have traveled as far as Detroit Michigan to go to slams. **(8)** When the audience cheers for me I feel great.

Punctuation continued

Apostrophes

Use an apostrophe to show letters are missing in a contraction.
• aren't (are not), can't (cannot), haven't (have not).

Do not confuse contractions with possessives that sound like them. A possessive pronoun never has an apostrophe.

The cat licked <u>its</u> fur (the fur belonging to it), and now <u>it's</u> (contraction for *it is*) clean.

Also use an apostrophe to show possession.
• Cal's dad drives him to school. The students' days start early.

Exercise: Apostrophes

Fix the apostrophe mistake in each sentence.

(1) Javiers hobby is krumping. **(2)** Its a kind of dance. **(3)** Hes dancing with his friends now. **(4)** The dancer's channel their energy into their moves. **(5)** Theyre very fit.

Quotation Marks

Use quotation marks before and after someone's exact words. Do not use them to set off an indirect quotation.
Direct Quotation: "I'm ready," Shari said, "to work."
Indirect Quotation: Shari said she was ready to work.

Set off titles of articles, short stories, and episodes of TV shows with quotation marks.
Title of Essay: Did you read the article "Sports Shorts"?
Title of Story: My favorite story is "Amigo Brothers."

Exercise: Quotation Marks

Add quotation marks where needed in the sentences below.

1. Did you study for the history quiz? Mark asked.

2. Laura said that she had read the article Patriots and Rebels.

3. I meant to study, said Chaz, but I fell asleep.

Spelling

Some words are spelled exactly the way they sound. Unfortunately, many are not. Use these rules to spell correctly. When in doubt, turn to a dictionary for help.

1. Put *i* before *e* except after *c* or in the sound *ay*.

Examples: c*ei*ling, rec*ei*pt, rec*ei*ve, fr*ei*ght, n*ei*ghbor, w*ei*ght

2. When adding an ending that starts with a vowel (like *-ed*, *-er*, or *-ing*), double these final consonants: *b, d, g, l, m, n, p, r,* and *t*.

Examples: sob*bed*, nag*ged*, begin*ner*, win*ner*, tap*ping*, bat*ting*

3. When adding *-ed*, *-es*, *-ing*, or *-y* to a word that ends with a silent *e*, drop the *e*.

Examples: create + *-ed* = creat*ed*, amaze + *-es* = amaz*es*, dazzle + *-ing* = dazz*ling*, tape + *-ing* = tap*ing*, rose + *y* = ros*y*

4. When a word ends in a consonant plus *y*, change the *y* to *i* before adding an ending like *-ed*, *-es*, *-est*, or *-ly*.

Examples: supply + *-ed* = suppl*ied*, fly + *-es* = flies, easy + *-est* = eas*iest*, happy + *ly* = happ*ily*

5. When a word ends in a vowel plus *y*, do not change the *y* to *i* when adding *-ed*, *-er*, or *-s*.

Examples: delayed, player, rays, says, keys, toys, guys

Exercise: Spelling

Highlight and fix the spelling mistake in each sentence.

(1) Coach, did you recieve the shipment of shoes for the soccer team? **(2)** Did you order the other supplys we need? **(3)** My nieghbor Lonny wants to play this year. **(4)** Last year, he played sloppyly. **(5)** This year, he amazeed me with his speed. **(6)** Also, Sal's footwork is dazzleing. **(7)** All the plaiers are ready for the season. **(8)** Some of the guyes have been training for months. **(9)** This will be the crazyest season ever for our team. **(10)** I predict that we'll be winers by December.

Commonly Confused Words

The words on this list give many writers trouble. Use the list for help in figuring out the right word to use.

accept, except
Accept means "to agree to" or "to welcome." *Except* means "but."

- I hope everyone will <u>accept</u> the new student to our class.
- We go to school every day <u>except</u> Saturday and Sunday.

affect, effect
Affect means "to influence" or "to have an impact on." *Effect* means "result."

- I hope the cancelled flight will not <u>affect</u> your travel plans.
- A high fever was one <u>effect</u> of the disease.

a lot
The expression *a lot* means "a large number" or "a large amount." It must be written as two words.

- <u>A lot</u> of people came to the championship game.

all ready, already
The expression *all ready* means "completely prepared." It is written as two words. *Already* means "previously" or "before now." It is one word.

- Dinner was <u>all ready</u> by the time the guests arrived.
- I got to the stadium so late the game was <u>already</u> over.

amount, number
The term *amount* describes a quantity that cannot be counted. Use *number* to describe a total of items that can be counted.

- The cake contained a large <u>amount</u> of sugar.
- She was impressed by the <u>number</u> of tickets that were sold.

beside, besides
Beside refers to someone or something "alongside" another. *Besides* means "as well as" or "other than."

- She stood <u>beside</u> the lamppost, waiting for the bus.
- <u>Besides</u> math, I also like to study science and English.

Commonly Confused Words continued

can, may

The word *can* means "is able." *May* means "is permitted."

- She <u>can</u> repair the car, because she has the right tools.
- He <u>may</u> watch the concert because he has a ticket.

fewer, less

Fewer compares numbers of people or things that can be counted. *Less* compares amounts or quantities that cannot be counted.

- The class had <u>fewer</u> boys than girls.
- My new car uses <u>less</u> gas than my old one.

like, as

Like is a preposition, and it should be followed by an object. *As* is a conjunction, and it should be followed by a clause, which contains both a subject and a verb.

- She sings <u>like</u> a bird.
- She sings <u>as</u> a bird would sing.

loose, lose

Loose is an adjective (meaning "weakly connected" or "unattached"), or it is a verb (meaning "set free" or "untied"). *Lose* is always a verb (meaning the opposite of "to win" or "to find").

- The <u>loose</u> stones in the wall fell to the street.
- The team that does not practice is sure to <u>lose</u> the game.

rise, raise

Rise means "to go up." *Raise* is used with an object, and it means "to lift or force."

- Please <u>raise</u> your hand if you have a question.
- The sun will <u>rise</u> at seven o'clock tomorrow morning.

sit, set

Sit means "to be seated." *Set* means "to put or place."

- I will <u>sit</u> at the table during dinner.
- I will <u>set</u> the dishes on the table.

Commonly Confused Words continued

than, then

Than is a conjunction used to compare one person or thing with another. *Then* is an adverb that means "after that" or " next."
- An elephant is larger <u>than</u> a mouse.
- First beat the eggs and <u>then</u> add the milk.

their, there, they're

Their is a possessive pronoun, which is used to show that something belongs to someone. *They're* is the contraction of *they* and *are*. Use *there* to express where something is.
- <u>They're</u> going to swim during <u>their</u> visit to Florida.
- The weather is sunny and warm <u>there</u>.

to, too, two

To expresses direction or location. *Too* means "as well" or "in addition." *Two* is the number between one and three.
- I bought <u>two</u> tickets for the concert, so you can come, <u>too</u>.
- We should take a bus <u>to</u> the theater.

who, whom

Who is the subject of the verb that follows it. *Whom* is an object, either receiving the action of a verb or ending a prepositional phrase.
- <u>Who</u> wrote the letter?
- To <u>whom</u> did you write the letter?

who's, whose

Who's is a contraction meaning "who is." *Whose* is a possessive pronoun, expressing ownership or relationship.
- <u>Who's</u> going to be our teacher next year?
- Do you know <u>whose</u> bicycle this is?

Editing Checklist

Use this checklist as you edit your writing. (You can also use this checklist to edit a partner's work.) Keep track as you complete each step.

1. I found misspelled words and used strategies to spell them correctly.

2. I checked to be sure that I used the correct homophone, such as *your/you're*, *to/too/two*, and *they're/their/there*.

3. I reread each sentence to make sure that I did not leave out words.

4. I fixed run-on sentences and sentence fragments.

5. I looked to be sure that each new idea started a new paragraph.

6. I correctly placed periods, question marks, exclamation marks, and commas where they belong.

7. I began each sentence with an uppercase letter.

8. I used uppercase letters for names of people and places and for proper nouns.

9. I made sure that subjects and verbs in sentences agree.

My editing goals:

_____

_____

_____

_____

_____

_____

Proofreaders' Marks

Use these marks as you review your own or a partner's writing.

୭	Delete	∧	Insert here
◡	Close up; delete space	⋀	Insert comma
(stet)	Let it stand	⌄	Insert apostrophe
#	Insert space	⌄⌄	Insert quotation marks
¶	Begin new paragraph	⊙	Insert period
(sp)	Spell out	(set)?	Insert question mark
(lc)	Set in lowercase	⌄	Insert colon
(caps)	Set in capital letters	=	Insert hyphen

Dear Jurors⋀

I think you should put you're trust in forensic science⊙

One reason for is that a witness to a crime may not

rember all the details. Proove from science is reliable. its

hard to argue with a fingerprint or dna Another reason

is that science keeps getting gooder. Compared to a

long time ago scientists can find out more information୭

About crime scenes. If you were accused of a crime,

wouldn't you want science on your side⌄

Personal Word Bank

Use the Word Bank to keep track of the "Your Choice" words from the articles.

For each word you add, do the following:

- Write the word in the box.
- Rate how well you understand it.

  1 = I do not know this word.

  2 = I have seen or heard this word.

  3 = I could use this word in a sentence.

  4 = I could teach this word to someone else.

- Write the definition in your own words.
- Write an example of the word or a connection you have with it.
- Use the word! Write with it, speak with it, and pay attention if you find it in your reading. Then go back to your rating and see if you can improve it.

Word: _____	My Understanding 1 2 3 4	Word: _____	My Understanding 1 2 3 4
Definition: _____		Definition: _____	
Example or Connection: _____		Example or Connection: _____	

Word: _____	My Understanding 1 2 3 4	Word: _____	My Understanding 1 2 3 4
Definition: _____		Definition: _____	
Example or Connection: _____		Example or Connection: _____	

Word: _____	My Understanding 1 2 3 4	Word: _____	My Understanding 1 2 3 4
Definition: _____		Definition: _____	
Example or Connection: _____		Example or Connection: _____	

Personal Word Bank

Word: _____ | My Understanding 1 2 3 4

Definition: _____

Example or Connection: _____
_____
_____

Word: _____ | My Understanding 1 2 3 4

Definition: _____

Example or Connection: _____
_____
_____

Word: _____ | My Understanding 1 2 3 4

Definition: _____

Example or Connection: _____
_____
_____

Word: _____ | My Understanding 1 2 3 4

Definition: _____

Example or Connection: _____
_____
_____

Word: _____ | My Understanding 1 2 3 4

Definition: _____

Example or Connection: _____
_____
_____

Word: _____ | My Understanding 1 2 3 4

Definition: _____

Example or Connection: _____
_____
_____

Word: _____ | My Understanding 1 2 3 4

Definition: _____

Example or Connection: _____
_____
_____

Word: _____ | My Understanding 1 2 3 4

Definition: _____

Example or Connection: _____
_____
_____

Word: _____ | My Understanding 1 2 3 4

Definition: _____

Example or Connection: _____
_____
_____

Word: _____ | My Understanding 1 2 3 4

Definition: _____

Example or Connection: _____
_____
_____

Personal Word Bank

Word: _____	My Understanding 1 2 3 4

Definition: _____

Example or Connection: _____

_____

_____

Word: _____	My Understanding 1 2 3 4

Definition: _____

Example or Connection: _____

_____

_____

Word: _____	My Understanding 1 2 3 4

Definition: _____

Example or Connection: _____

_____

_____

Word: _____	My Understanding 1 2 3 4

Definition: _____

Example or Connection: _____

_____

_____

Word: _____	My Understanding 1 2 3 4

Definition: _____

Example or Connection: _____

_____

_____

Word: _____	My Understanding 1 2 3 4

Definition: _____

Example or Connection: _____

_____

_____

Word: _____	My Understanding 1 2 3 4

Definition: _____

Example or Connection: _____

_____

_____

Word: _____	My Understanding 1 2 3 4

Definition: _____

Example or Connection: _____

_____

_____

Word: _____	My Understanding 1 2 3 4

Definition: _____

Example or Connection: _____

_____

_____

Word: _____	My Understanding 1 2 3 4

Definition: _____

Example or Connection: _____

_____

_____

Personal Word Bank

Word: _____	My Understanding 1 2 3 4

Definition: _____

Example or Connection: _____
_____
_____

Word: _____	My Understanding 1 2 3 4

Definition: _____

Example or Connection: _____
_____
_____

Word: _____	My Understanding 1 2 3 4

Definition: _____

Example or Connection: _____
_____
_____

Word: _____	My Understanding 1 2 3 4

Definition: _____

Example or Connection: _____
_____
_____

Word: _____	My Understanding 1 2 3 4

Definition: _____

Example or Connection: _____
_____
_____

Word: _____	My Understanding 1 2 3 4

Definition: _____

Example or Connection: _____
_____
_____

Word: _____	My Understanding 1 2 3 4

Definition: _____

Example or Connection: _____
_____
_____

Word: _____	My Understanding 1 2 3 4

Definition: _____

Example or Connection: _____
_____
_____

Word: _____	My Understanding 1 2 3 4

Definition: _____

Example or Connection: _____
_____
_____

Word: _____	My Understanding 1 2 3 4

Definition: _____

Example or Connection: _____
_____
_____

Personal Word Bank

Word: _____ | My Understanding
Definition: _____
Example or Connection: _____

Word: _____ | My Understanding
Definition: _____
Example or Connection: _____

Word: _____ | My Understanding
Definition: _____
Example or Connection: _____

Word: _____ | My Understanding
Definition: _____
Example or Connection: _____

Word: _____ | My Understanding
Definition: _____
Example or Connection: _____

Word: _____ | My Understanding
Definition: _____
Example or Connection: _____

Word: _____ | My Understanding
Definition: _____
Example or Connection: _____

Word: _____ | My Understanding
Definition: _____
Example or Connection: _____

Word: _____ | My Understanding
Definition: _____
Example or Connection: _____

Word: _____ | My Understanding
Definition: _____
Example or Connection: _____

Personal Word Bank

Word: _____	My Understanding 1 2 3 4

Definition: _____

Example or Connection: _____

_____

_____

Word: _____	My Understanding 1 2 3 4

Definition: _____

Example or Connection: _____

_____

_____

Word: _____	My Understanding 1 2 3 4

Definition: _____

Example or Connection: _____

_____

_____

Word: _____	My Understanding 1 2 3 4

Definition: _____

Example or Connection: _____

_____

_____

Word: _____	My Understanding 1 2 3 4

Definition: _____

Example or Connection: _____

_____

_____

Word: _____	My Understanding 1 2 3 4

Definition: _____

Example or Connection: _____

_____

_____

Word: _____	My Understanding 1 2 3 4

Definition: _____

Example or Connection: _____

_____

_____

Word: _____	My Understanding 1 2 3 4

Definition: _____

Example or Connection: _____

_____

_____

Word: _____	My Understanding 1 2 3 4

Definition: _____

Example or Connection: _____

_____

_____

Word: _____	My Understanding 1 2 3 4

Definition: _____

Example or Connection: _____

_____

_____